Multiculturalism in Waldorf Education

Printed with support from the Waldorf Curriculum Fund

Published by:
Waldorf Publications at the
Research Institute for Waldorf Education
38 Main Street
Chatham, NY 12037

Title: *Multiculturalism in Waldorf Education*
Edited by: Waldorf Multicultural Committee

Reprinted from Issues 1–3, 1990–1993
ISBN# 978-1-936367-85-6
© October 2015
Proofreader, copy editor: Melissa Merkling
Layout: Ann Erwin

Cover image: Originally created for an Apocalypse conference
by Charles Andrade, artist in the Washington, DC, area

Multiculturalism in Waldorf Education

Waldorf Multicultural Committee
1990–1993

Table of Contents

I, too, sing America.

I am the darker brother.
They send me to eat in the kitchen
When company comes,
But I laugh,
And eat well,
And grow strong.

Tomorrow,
I'll be at the table
When company comes.
Nobody'll dare
Say to me,
"Eat in the kitchen,"
Then.

Besides,
They'll see how beautiful I am
And be ashamed —

I, too, am America.

–Langston Hughes

from *American Negro Poetry*,
ed. by Arna Bontemps,
New York: Hill and Wang, 1963

Foreword

Cultural sensibilities change over time. Words used casually may sound offensive once consciousness is informed and awakened to a topic. Indeed these very same words can be helpful in raising consciousness to new awareness. The words themselves may not alter the inner feelings of an individual, but the recasting of their meanings in terms of contemporary parlance can make us all the more aware of the underlying concerns for human dignity that can inspire feelings of uplift or harm, depending upon how the words are used and who expresses them.

The following pages were published as a newsletter in three volumes during the early 1990s. The Milwaukee public school project and the opening of the first charter schools drew attention to some of the limits inherent in the vocabulary surrounding independent Waldorf education. Especially in the domain of African-American culture, the language of Waldorf schools in North America had become Eurocentric and, perhaps by accident or oversight, may have sounded less inclusive than what was intended or even practiced in the independent Waldorf schools.

The authors of these studies and reports on multiculturalism, formulated between 1990 and 1993, worked to educate us about the rich culture and history of Africans in America. Their intention was to forge more open and informed language and through this language to pioneer a more inclusive approach to the ways we teach and address each other.

Here combined are the three reports that were completed by this dedicated group of Waldorf teachers. We publish them with the intention of sparking additional study of the issues of racism and classism still alive in North American culture, especially as it relates to Hispanics, Latinos, Asians, and people of Southwest Asian descent.

We are publishing these reports as a book in the spirit of the original researchers, who upheld with openhearted courage a picture of the universal human being that underlies all of Waldorf education, wherever it is practiced in the world. In this sense it is our wish that the dream might be realized that was articulated by Martin Luther King, Jr., who prayed that children might live one day in "a nation where they will not be judged by the color of their skin, but by the content of their character."

– Patrice Maynard
Chatham, New York
Saint Martin's 2015

Multiculturalism in Waldorf Education

Awakening to America's Need

The following article was written in part by East Bay Waldorf parent Che Norman and Seattle Waldorf class teacher Keith Jefferson as the task of the Multicultural Committee. The group seeks to identify the research and process by which a broader (i.e., multicultural) inclusiveness may become a vital aspect of Waldorf education in the United States. Moreover, the group will examine attitudes, stereotypes and cultural biases that may prohibit the wider participation of "people of color" in our educational movement. The seven questions Ms. Norman lists in her article are merely initial forays into this realm of unique importance to all Americans. Subsequent reports will further clarify each question and hopefully provide practical ways in which individuals may deepen their awareness.

A Valentine for the Other Americans

On a clear but brisk Valentine's Day evening during the February Teachers' Conference in Fair Oaks, a small group gathered in the Rudolf Steiner College science room to look at the future of Waldorf education in America from a unique perspective. The gathering included parents, teacher trainees, and teachers representing a cluster of Northern California schools as well as Seattle, Vermont and Vancouver. What we specifically had in common was our commitment to anthroposophy/Waldorf education and our heightened concerns over the alarming invisibility of "people of color" (this phrase is the preferred description of American non-white minorities) in our schools. In our parent bodies, teaching and administrative staffs, teacher training programs, and, most troubling, in our classrooms, Native, African, Hispanic, Latino, and Asian Americans are conspicuously absent—this, in an educational system some sixty years in existence in America. That evening this small group began to look at this phenomenon, beginning by sharing aspects of their biographies that helped to shed light on exactly why this theme had relevance for them.

Che Norman, African-American mother of four, two of whom are students at the East Bay Waldorf School near Berkeley, brings an insight and compassion to her experiences (and those of her daughter) that are a window into our schools that few have had an opportunity to look through. Her thoughts are at once a challenge and a reminder to us all that the ideals proffered by Waldorf education still struggle to become our ideals.

Notes from a Black Waldorf Mother

After researching most of the private schools in the San Francisco Bay Area, it was clear that Waldorf education was the only option for my children. I sensed immediately that the school provided a loving and spiritual environment with a humanistic base.

However, after four years as a Waldorf parent, I am very saddened by many things that I do not see. The few Waldorf schools I have seen all feel to me as if they were just transported in a bubble from Europe, with all the ethnocentric trappings that go along with it. For example, our school store was a delightful, colorful place with beautiful handmade dolls—all fair-skinned; lovely fairy tale stories—all with fair-skinned, rosy-cheeked children on the covers; wonderful white angels hung gently in the air—a lovely place that did not include me or my children. An unintentionally closed environment. I'm happy to say that this is beginning to change. There is more variety in the book selections, and our special request that dolls and gnomes be made in a variety of skin tones has been met. All of this makes the store (which is often the first thing visitors see) much more inviting to all. This is but one example of how change can take place.

After finding her crying in her room one day, I asked my six-year-old daughter what was wrong. What she said broke my heart. "Mommy, why are all the angels at school always white? Are there no black angels in heaven?" Although it's not my first choice, my daughter can survive being the only black child in her class, but I don't think she can survive never seeing images of herself, hearing stories she can relate to and living daily with rituals that include only white angels, white gnomes, white princes and princesses. She cannot survive being ignored.

I've invited many friends to see the school. So many have commented that, although they loved the school, they sensed that it was not a place that cared to include their non-white children.

My concerns, however, spread wider than that. I work with my children at home, in many ways, to boost their self-image and knowledge of who they are. But what of all the white children in the Waldorf schools who see little of present-day cultures in their classrooms and have little or no contact with people of other cultures? I believe they are the bigger losers.

We want our children to have an education based on wholeness, yet they are in an environment that is strongly based on European concepts that often fail to acknowledge the gifts from other cultures. Waldorf education in the United States has a large challenge to meet. This is not Europe. We have the privilege of living in a society that is wonderfully diverse. The opportunities to grow and expand are almost endless. It is no longer enough to be non-racist. Now is a time to move deliberately toward total inclusiveness. This requires that we all come out of our own little worlds and wake up!

We are losing children and teachers of color faster than we can take them in. This is a terrible loss for all Waldorf schools. Our school, in the East Bay, feels like a community. We all work hard together to keep the school going. We all know how hard the teachers work while wearing their many, many hats. If changes are going to be addressed, we must do it together. Our education towards wholeness will not be whole otherwise.

Questions and Concerns

How can we develop resources and a curriculum appropriate to the Waldorf curriculum?

How can we attract more teachers of color?

How can the traditional teacher training expand to include multi-ethnic sensitivities with a diversity of resources?

How can we become more sensitive to persons of color in our school communities ?

How can we address questions from students of color? What are the special needs?

How can we make Waldorf education more accessible to students of color?

How do we understand anthroposophy in relation to multi-cultural education?

These questions are large in scope, but must be addressed … with an open heart and an open mind. Those of us who attended this meeting and the many who have expressed interest in this work since are excited about looking for the answers.

Thoughts on Waldorf Education and the Multicultural Focus

Betty Staley

Introduction

During the first months of my Waldorf teacher training in 1959, I addressed a burning question to Francis Edmunds: "How does this wonderful curriculum, developed for the child of central Europe, and then adapted for the English child, relate to the children of America?" He gave two answers. First, he told me to address myself to the archetypal question behind the curriculum, relate it to child development, and find the appropriate material out of the culture in which the child lives. Second, he said, "That is your task, Betty." For the last thirty years I have lived with the question and the two answers. Finally I believe the time is right to ask this question, not as an individual teacher concerned with the children and subject matter in an individual classroom, but as a question that should concern our entire North American Waldorf educational movement.

Waldorf education serves the spirit of the age, Michael, addressed to children of the consciousness soul age, relating to the challenges which confront the human spirit, arising out of a changing technological, information-oriented society, and arising out of the dynamic relationship between the teachers, children, and parents in a particular school. The beauty and uniqueness of Waldorf education is its ability to be universal and local at the same time because it understands the child to be born into a particular family and folk while at the same time being born into the human race. In other words, in its being, the child lives between the world of spirit and his or her own physical organism. The child relates to the universal spirit, on one hand, and the physical surroundings, on the other. In between is the whole world of soul—the world of feelings, the world of interactions between the experience of being human and the experience of being Chinese, Indian, Italian or American. The path to the universal human is through the folk, just as the path to universal love is first awakened through the love of the people closest to the child: the parents. In order for the teacher to understand the child, it is essential to understand the being of the child within his or her environment.

> [T]he point is not to think out some way in which a number of children may be educated quite apart from the world, according to one's own intellectual, abstract ideas, but rather to discover how children may be helped to grow into true human beings within the social milieu which is their environment. One must muster one's strength and not take children away from the social milieu in which they are living. It is essential to have this courage. It is something which is connected with the world significance of education.[1]

Many times in the educational lectures, Rudolf Steiner stresses how important it is for the teachers to get to know the children they are teaching. This deep interest is a healing in our times.

Whoever has the gift for observing such things can experience how sometimes teachers who have thoroughly mastered educational theories, who can recount admirably everything they had to know for their examination, or had to learn in practice class-teaching, nevertheless remain utterly removed from life when they come face to face with the children they have to teach. What has happened to such a teacher is what, daily and hourly, we are forced to observe with a sorrowing heart, the fact that people pass one another by in life, that they have no sense of getting to know one another. This is a common state of affairs. It is the fundamental evil which underlies all social disturbances which are so widespread in the cultural life of today: the lack of paying heed to others, the lack of interest which every man should have for others. In everyday civilized life we must perforce accept such a state of affairs; it is the destiny of modern humanity at the present time.[2]

Just as the answers expressed in Waldorf education in 1919 in Central Europe addressed the needs of children who existed then and there, new answers have to express themselves in Waldorf education today in America. The central question relates to an understanding of the folk-soul. What is the American folk soul and how does the Waldorf curriculum address this?

There is already so much in the Waldorf curriculum that awakens the child's understanding of the journey of the human soul in world history. We have only to wake up to it. But then there are other areas where it is not a matter of taking an "Ur-curriculum" and adapting it, adjusting it, so that we feel we are compromising. Quite the opposite, the process is one of entering into the direct experience of the child and co-creating what is needed to meet the child's soul. This is not compromise.

The American folk-soul is unique. It is not clearly defined the way the Russian or English folk-soul is. Some even say America does not really have a folk-soul, but that it is giving birth to a new folk-soul, not to be a carbon copy of the folk-souls of people who settled in this land, but to be something that we cannot yet identify. It will arise alchemically out of the furnace of the past but possessing the spark of the new.

There is a great opportunity to develop something new in human history here in the West. On one hand, there is the promise of freedom, unhampered by past traditions. This leaves us free to develop what needs to become. Yet, on the other, there is rootlessness. The past is always slipping away, and it is very difficult to hold on to traditions or to imbue them with substance. Are American folk traditions the traditions brought by our forefathers from the countries of their origin? Are we all hyphenated Americans? Or is "American" all of these and none of these?

What is the relation of the American folk-soul to the Native American who revered the earth, knowing full well it was the mother of us all? What is the relation of the American folk-soul to the Chinese who were brought over to work in the gold mines and to lay track for the railroads? Or the boat people who have made their way from Southeast Asia to our shores during this decade? What is the relation of the American folk-soul to the

Africans who were separated from their families, sold at market, and brought to work the fields of cotton, tobacco, and sugar cane? What is the relation of each of us to the American folk-soul? These questions should form the basis of our research as Waldorf teachers as we try to understand the children we teach.

A group of Waldorf teachers and parents has come together to form the Waldorf Multicultural Committee to begin addressing many of these questions as they refer to our education. This is a committee open to any who feel the interest in working with these issues. We have taken as our first task the examination of the way we address Black culture in our schools. We hope to inspire groups around the country to concentrate on other aspects of American culture so that we can provide resources to teachers and develop a better understanding of how Waldorf education can meet the people of this land. Our purpose is not to be nationalistic, but to understand the folk-soul in which we live so that we may experience it consciously and appreciate it. From that experience, our children can experience themselves as world citizens.

Addressing the African-American Aspect of Our Culture

I often ask myself, why were Black people brought to this country as slaves? What qualities do the Africans have in their makeup that the Europeans needed in order to meet in this new environment?

Without becoming lost in stereotypes, it is possible to say that Northern European culture, which makes up such a strong part of the American population, lives in its thinking, lives out of its mental processes, thus bypassing the heart and moving directly into the will. This can develop into one-sidedness. In the same way, African culture can be characterized as emerging from the heart, bypassing the thinking and moving directly into the will. It, too, can be one-sided. This does not mean that Europeans don't feel and Africans don't think. It means that there is an inner experience from which the individual meets the world. Out of the meeting of the two experiences—here in a new environment—a healthy, balanced experience of thinking, feeling, and willing can arise which can bring about a new possibility.

We need each other. Our history, unfortunately, has been fraught with incidents which deny basic respect and appreciation to our Black sisters and brothers. They have been denied human dignity. They have been judged from a one-sided viewpoint. Our inability to understand this has resulted in the tragedy that besets Black America today and is eating away at the heart of America. The detriment is to Black and White alike. It is to us all as human beings.

How does this relate to Waldorf education?

When Rudolf Steiner developed the Threefold Social Impulse, he was attempting to meet the situation in Central Europe in the post-World War I years. A neutral, healing middle was needed between the impulses of Moscow and Washington, as they were beginning to emerge as world powers.

> ... a new social order in which the economic and
> political life should not be the only dominant factor;

a free cultural-spiritual life should be fostered, which would bring new forces into existence.[3]

Waldorf education was the answer to the needs of the time. It still is. The need to develop a new social order in which the free cultural-spiritual life would be fostered is only in its infancy. Yet the way it answers that need will be different in each geographical region. In this context we must ask ourselves: What is the task of Waldorf education in America?

Whereas Central Europe lies between Moscow and Washington, America lies between Europe and Africa to the east and Asia to the west, between Canada in the north and Latin America to the south. Influences in America are from north and south as well as from east and west. Here we have a crossing point where the various streams interact and influence each other. Rather than a folk-consciousness arising out of these various streams, a new consciousness, a world consciousness must arise, serving the cosmopolitan impulse of Michael. Michael stands for heart-warmed thinking, active thinking which unites spirit and will and transforms.

A consideration of this issue becomes relevant in a practical way when we start discussing curriculum. From the first grade where fairy tales are introduced and the fables and legends of the second grade, to the myths of the next grades and the biographies of the upper grades, we must make conscious decisions about which examples to choose.

For example, for sixteen years I have taught art history to ninth graders. This course traces art from the ancient world through the 17th century in Europe, climaxing with the work of Rembrandt. This is basically a course introducing the student to the journey of Western civilization, through the examples of art representing the sentient soul, intellectual soul, and consciousness soul. The art represented is mostly European (except for the study of ancient Egypt). This journey is very important. But it is not enough. Where does the American student learn about American art, arising out of the interweaving of the Native American, European, African, Hispanic, and Oriental cultures— all of which make up America? Although it may be added on to a course here and there, it does not play a central role in the curriculum at present.

The same situation exists in history, literature and music. The world is seen through European eyes. This is not a fault of our European colleagues. They were developing schools for European children. But it is our task as American Waldorf teachers to address this, and to this point in time we have made only feeble beginnings. For example, in California, by the year 2000 the majority of people will be people of color. How will our curriculum take this into consideration ?

Many times since 1959, I have addressed this issue to my colleagues here in America. Basically, we have avoided the question. It is 70 years since the founding of the first Waldorf school; the first Waldorf school in North America opened its doors in New York in 1928. This is its 63rd year here. In Rudolf Steiner's insights into the human biography, he speaks of a person becoming free of past destiny around the age of 63. We should be ever grateful to our European colleagues for all that they have done to preserve and strengthen Waldorf education. There is much work we have to do together as Waldorf education continues to develop as a world movement. In addition, we will not be able to relate our schools to American culture, understanding and acknowledging the place of each subject in the curriculum, until we recognize, with respect and love, the contributions of Black Americans. As we do this, we will be joined by many more African-Americans who wish to be Waldorf teachers. We will receive many more African-American families into our schools. Most important, students of all colors will benefit as they become much more familiar with the literature and history of African-Americans.

Our children are creating the future. When we more consciously take on the task of integrating African-American culture into our work, Waldorf education will act as a transformative element in American society.

ENDNOTES

1. Rudolf Steiner, *Human Values in Education* (Arnhem, Holland 1924), London: Rudolf Steiner Press, 1971.
2. Ibid., p. 16.
3. Carl Stegmann, "Rudolf Steiner Shows a Way Out of Chaos, Part I"; from *America in the Threefold World,* Study Letter Number X, December 20, 1984, p. 8.

Black Culture, South Africa and the New Surge Toward Freedom

How Will Waldorf Education Respond?

Keith Jefferson

This article was written for the Seattle Waldorf School newsletter, February 1986.

> … Whether 'tis nobler in the mind
> to suffer the slings and arrows of outrageous fortune
> or to take arms against a sea of troubles, and by opposing
> end them?—to die—to sleep—No more!
>> – *Hamlet*, Act III, Scene I
>> William Shakespeare

We just celebrated the first nationally recognized observation of the birthday of the late Dr. Martin Luther King, Jr., whose distinguished career was cut short by an assassin's bullet in Memphis, Tennessee, over twenty years ago. During last year's observation, I wanted to bring a fresh, yet meaningful picture to our children. Despite the fact that we have only a smattering of Black children in the school, the message of Dr. King is, nevertheless, something everyone should be able to understand regardless of race. But what particular picture for these particular kids? I came across the idea of using the myth of Orpheus and his harp. The story of Orpheus and his calming of a raging beast with the soothing heartfelt tones of music seemed an apt and timeless metaphor for the essence of Dr. King's strivings. The children were enraptured with the Orpheus story and seemed to make the transition with me easily to the struggle of Dr. King and what he represented.

Dr. King and countless other African and African-American personalities are under particular attention during the yearly celebrations of Black History Month, an official remembrance during the month of February of the struggles and triumphs of Blacks. The noted historian and educator, Carter G. Woodson, often referred to as the "Father of Black American History," was instrumental in founding this event.

Growing up in an all-Black community as a youngster, I remember February as a time when regular school course study was highlighted by the adventures of Harriet Tubman, the poetry of James Weldon Johnson and Langston Hughes, and even the music of Leadbelly, Paul Robeson and the Dixie Hummingbirds. It seemed quirkily out-of-date stuff for the mildly streetwise Black youth of the mid-50s but it certainly helped to widen the perspectives of the world mostly available to us through the decidedly suburban adventures of Dick and Jane and the antics of Peanuts and Jocko in our Weekly Readers.

I would venture to say that such a celebration plays a quite minimal role in the cultural life of today's American Waldorf schools—that is to say, if it has any impact at all. I state this knowing that if there were more schools with considerable Black student populations (the Detroit Waldorf School comes to mind), such an observation would no doubt be a more obvious consideration. Within the scope of the Waldorf teaching curriculum I find there is incredible room for personal initiative, limited only by the individual teacher's breadth of life experience and creative resources. My question then is, what happens in all the other Waldorf schools in America that are patently unlike a Detroit school? What happens when the likelihood that through tuition rates, location and various and sundry reasons, the minority (in this case, Black) population is conspicuous through its absence? Can these excuses justify a cultural no-show in a contemporary U.S. school?

The situation is this: The national makeup of American Waldorf schools, now in their 57th year, has been and is overwhelmingly from white, middle-class to upper middle-class homes, including single-parent families. These children ask by their very composition for a kind of awakening, a gentle but consistent introduction to a more specific broadening than is perhaps available through the basic curriculum. There are numerous ways in which Black and African cultural elements could play more visible roles in our everyday work in Waldorf schools, especially from third grade onwards.

This, incidentally, is not an appeal for a Black studies program, but rather a reminder that a curriculum with a world-view can hardly afford to pay lip-service to a continent and its people. What is ironic is that so much attention has been centered on the plight of the various African peoples North and South this year. My third grade class, largely through the TV news media, has sat through nightly vignettes of mass starvation and disease in Ethiopia and Chad as well as scenes of pitched battles between young, school-age Black South Africans and heavily armed White Afrikaaner police—scenes which, if I didn't know were Soweto mid-80s, I'd swear were Selma in the mid-60s. The third graders were abuzz with such questions as, "Isn't there any food in Africa, Mr. Jefferson?" and "How did it happen, Mr. Jefferson? Why are all the Black people dying?" and "Can't we send food there?" The reactions, hearteningly, were less recoils of horror and guilt but more a series of honest, concerned questions, an effort to make some sort of childlike sense of a complex series of plagues both natural and man-made. Later that week, a group of girls collected frozen ice crystals with painstaking care from the playground and sold them to teachers, parents, and each other. The three-or-so dollars collected were dutifully sent to an African famine relief organization by a very concerned first grader.

South Africa

This photograph is, to my knowledge, of the first all Black (or all Native, as is the Afrikaaner term) Waldorf school in the world. The Max Stibbe school in Transvaal-Pretoria is a bold and timely event of the spirit. Given the growing bitterness and violence in South Africa as of late, it is ironic that such an event as a school based on the ideas of Rudolf Steiner should be available to a primarily Black township—these communities where the words "freedom" and "equality" are by no means taken lightly. Now more than at any other time or in any other place does

Eurythmy class at the Max Stibbe School in South Africa

Steiner's often quoted aim of true education take on startling and specific meaning: "Our highest endeavor must be to develop free human beings who are able of themselves to impart purpose and direction to their lives."

There is no doubt that the long and deeply inhuman reign of the Afrikaaner government is staring into the sunset of its control of the lives of the Black South African. The question is not only how this will happen (the prospects are chilling) but what will the nature of that society be afterwards? This is where the influence of children, perhaps by that time young adults, who have grown to see the world as a unified whole, behind which an integrated benevolence lives and breathes, will be of utmost importance.

Tribal songs from Zulu and Xhosa culture have long been staple elements in the Johannesburg and Cape Town Waldorf schools even if the children of those cultures could not attend those schools. Doubtless this is a small and perhaps in the larger scale a relatively non-threatening concession, but consider this. Here in America where there has not been a major racial uprising for nearly a generation, what is the impetus for including Pan-African experiences in our work with our children? Or is there any need beyond the festivities surrounding Black History Month?

These are questions each American Waldorf teacher should ask him- or herself, for in the long struggle towards true humanity, certain ignorances are hardly blissful—racism is without a doubt one of them, as is indifference. I recall a very interesting lecture by Laurens van der Post, author of *The Lost World of the Kalahari*, who is South African-born and a keen and compassionate observer of the plight of the African. Mr. van der Post also happens to be a lifelong student of Rudolf Steiner's work, and in a lecture he gave at the Waldorf School in Adelphi University in 1963, he stated by way of summing up a parable in relation to the South African situation: If you accept your neighbor's heresy, his failing, as part of your own, you can both snap out of it. I think there is hope, because we in South Africa, not all of us, but a great many people on all four sides, since there are also colored and Indian peoples there, see the problem as part of the raw material of life which we must transcend by our own personal example.

Mr. van der Post concludes by saying:

If I am not entirely hopeless, it's because we could put
things right in South Africa, if the world outside were to
see its troubles in the same light and help by its example.

The dreams of a Dr. Martin Luther King, Jr., the harsh realities
of a South African township—these are constant reminders that
the price of freedom can never be too high for the human spirit
to pay. As Waldorf teachers we must be aware that when we
"imbue ourselves with the power of imagination, have courage
for the truth, and sharpen our feelings for responsibility of soul,"
we consciously take on a spiritual brotherhood with the peoples
of the world. To our children, we are examples of the highest
cosmopolitan efforts of the world spirits. In us, in our thoughts
and actions, the fortune of human destiny loses its outrage and
becomes—in Hamlet's words, "… a consummation of the flesh,
devoutly to be wished."

Children of John Henry

Notes on African-American Culture
and the Waldorf Curriculum

Keith Jefferson

This article was written in February, 1990, four years after the preceding one. It, too, was written for the Seattle Waldorf School newsletter.

> In America the living together of the representatives of the whole of humanity in one fold demands the quest for a spirit of the whole of humanity who can unite all peoples.[1]   – Carl Stegmann

> [T]he double obligation of being both Negro and American is not so unified as we are often led to believe.
> – Countee Cullen, Harlem Renaissance poet

> We [Europeans)] have developed a culture primarily through our mental powers; in African civilization the heart predominates.[2]
> – Dr. L.F.C. Mees

Within the archetypal characteristics of the pulsating heart of the human being lie the elements that are akin to the mood of the African-American: rhythm, warmth, tempo and beat.

Many are the children's hand-games from turn-of-the-century Northern inner city ghettos, for example:

> Little Sally Walker
> sitting in a saucer
> weepin' and cryin'
> for someone to love her.
> Rise Sally rise
> go wipe your weepin' eyes
> Aw shake it to the East
> Aw shake it the West
> Shake it to the one you love the best.[3]

Or there is "Mary Mack," to which countless varieties of hand-clapping gestures have been wedded over the years.

> Oh Mary Mack, Mack, Mack
> All dressed in black, black, black
> With silver buttons, buttons, buttons
> All down her back, back, back.
> Well Heidi ho, ho, ho
> And Mary yo, yo, yo
> She got a needle, nccdle, needle,
> But she can't sew, sew, sew.[4]

In the rhythmical speech pattern of these and numerous other hand gesture/jump rope rhymes are the contrapuntal and polyrhythmical textures native to traditional and neo-African rhythms. First grade certainly isn't too early to introduce these elements during circle time or as a special treat during a games period. Simple seasonal Black Gospel or Sunday school songs like "Angels Watching Over Me," "Go Tell It On the Mountain," and "He's Got the Whole World In His Hands" are wonderfully warm picture-songs that many children already know from their family life. Older recordings by Mahalia Jackson, Ella Jenkins, the Staple Singers, Odetta, Josh White, Burl Ives, the Rev. Gary Davis, Pete Seeger, and the Weavers are great resources for such music.

The riddle-loving second grader would certainly appreciate the great wealth of riddles within traditional West African culture. A sampling:

A slender staff touches both Earth and Heaven.
Answer: Rainfall (Yoruba)

A fat wife, always busy and surrounded by a hedge
of thorns.
Answer: Tongue surrounded by teeth (Yoruba)

I have two brothers and sisters and cannot see either
of them.
Answer: Ears and eyes (Mende)[5]

Brought as a counterpoint to European riddles these are tiny mysteries that could take days of contemplation to solve.

The fables and animal stories that are so much a part of the second grade year in a Waldorf school open the door to a wide panorama of Black Southern American, traditional African, and Afro-Caribbean folk culture. The Anase spider stories are humorous and similar in contentual flavor to Kipling's Just-So stories.[6] Like Tom Thumb, Anase uses cleverness and his size to his ultimate advantage, while adventures like "How the Moon Came to Be in the Sky" and "How Spider Lost his Whiskers" give us a view into creation-myth symbology. Many Black historians have noted the remarkable similarities between the Anase spider character and another well-known American folk hero, Brer Rabbit.

Very few American Waldorf teachers whom I've talked to who have had second grade could resist the clever and zany adventures of Brer Rabbit, and indeed "Brer Rabbit and the Briar Patch" (including the Tar Baby, of course) is considered an American folk classic.[7]

However, on the question of whether or not Black vernacular dialect was used in telling the stories, there is often an embarrassed silence, a righteous "absolutely not" or a mumbled "I'd be horrible at that... ." In Joel Chandler Harris' lively collection of folk tales, Uncle Remus[8] becomes a larger-than-life literary figure who is a spokesman for the cumulative oral literature of the Black South. Harris' insistence on using the dialect of those from whom the stories were gleaned was an attempt to keep the mythic thread that held these stories together intact. Uncle Remus acts as a kind of New World "griot" (traditional West African seer mythologist)—the wise elder in whom reside the last vestiges of nature-clairvoyance. With his insatiably curious, little white charge in tow, Remus passes on these elemental proverbs, complete with a final act of power—the "Africanization" of the English language.

In his talks with Swiss Waldorf teachers in Basel in 1920, Rudolf Steiner stated that in observing dialect speakers, "…we soon become convinced that [children] speaking dialect have a more inward relationship to language than those who do not speak in dialect."

Steiner goes on to examine the relationship between dialect and mother tongue and states that it is "the result of experiencing the formation of words and the structure of sentences far more intensely and with a greater quality of Will than those who speak the so-called written language."[9]

I would venture to say that something infinitely deeper is relayed to the children through the conscious attempt at Black dialect in the Brer Rabbit stories than in all the episodes of the Cosby show put together. I encourage each second grade teacher to immerse himself or herself in this treasure chest of uniquely American neo-African Folk vernacular.

For third grade, from John Henry and onwards, the bedrock of Black community life from the earliest days of slavery in the American South has been the church. The most influential spokespeople for the Black condition and struggle in the U.S. have emerged into national and international recognition from the passionate embrace of the Black church (Rev. King, Rev. Ralph Abernathy from the Southern Christian Leadership Conference, Jesse Jackson from Chicago's Operation PUSH, to name a few).

In third grade the Old Testament plays a pivotal role in the academic year. Math, grammar, speech, dramatic plays, painting, drawing, and singing all have their source in the varied and colorful stories from the early books of the Bible. The parallel between the enslavement of the Hebrews under the yoke of the Pharaoh and the actual enslavement of Blacks in this country until the "Emancipation Proclamation" of 1863 is an obvious and soul-stirring one.

Much can be utilized from the countless Black gospel songs of the pre- and post-Emancipation South. The well-known "Go Down Moses" introduced at just the right moment during an Old Testament block on Moses and the plight of the Hebrews can be one of the most powerfully "correct" moments in one's teaching career.

In addition, work songs, chants, songs of the trades, field "hollers" and shouts that accompanied various farming and agricultural tasks are numerous and fun to learn. The rhythms are challenging but nonetheless infectious and perfectly made for clapping and stamping. Many of these gospel, secular songs display a typical African element: antiphony or "call and response." The leader or preacher calls out a verse and is countered by a class/congregation/group building up a strong breathing/rhythmical relationship. This lends itself wonderfully to the spirited metaphors of trial, hope, deliverance and freedom that this music so succinctly displays.

> Leader: Oh, the River of Jordan is deep and wide.
> Group: One more river to cross.
>
> Leader: I don't know how to get to the other side.
> Group: One more river to cross.[10]

The John Henry epic, for epic it has surely become, is one of the most well-known and powerful of all the folktales of the American South: a "common man" in contest with "the system," with technology, and with the very mountains that cast their daily shadows across the world in which common men and women live. The basic content of the story is simple: John Henry is a railroad laborer (with superhuman physical strength and endurance) who is convinced that no mechanical device such as a steam drill can ever replace a hard-working man in building a railroad. In an extraordinary race, pitting mechanical might against sheer human will, John Henry dies in the effort to prove his point.

The form in which this epic is found is as varied as the variations in the theme itself—blues, tragic ballad, worksong, washboard band air, lullaby, guitar and harmonica tunes, and prose narration. The exhilarating but tragic picture of human will and individual effort makes John Henry a likely candidate for the fourth grade curriculum. Henry's awesome feats of strength, even as a child, and his wielding of his 20-pound iron hammer give him a startling similarity to his willful, hammer-swinging counterpart in Norse mythology—Thor.

Many are the spiritually compelling elements in this decidedly secular myth: the premonition by the infant John Henry of his death; the willful intention to keep the machine technology at bay and in its proper relationship to human life; Henry's insistence on using pure iron hammers for what he called in one piece a "deeper strength"; and his relationship to his several "families." After John Henry's death in many renditions, his wife and children dutifully take up the work where he left off. Curiously enough, quite a few versions have the wife actually taking up John Henry's hammer and "drivin' piles" herself. Often she is called by the name Mary Magdalene.[11]

It is in the legacy of John Henry as archetype, and his connection with iron, and his morally articulated stance against the machine that a particularly Michaelic spark shines through. It is important to note that spiritual science tells us that one of the central tasks of America is to humanize technology in a way that makes the machine reflect the spiritual nature of the human being. In John Henry we have an authentic folk hero at once deeply American and yet connected to the leading spiritual powers of our age. We would do well to cultivate this powerful imagery, in some fashion, in our work in our schools. Is it not a blessing that such a Michaelic stream imagination exists, tempered, warmed and carried through within the African-American folk soul? Is not the legacy of John Henry a legacy for all Americans?

Conclusion

One article can hardly do justice to all the possibilities available to the teacher who attempts to broaden the curriculum along these impulses. There are West African housebuilding ideas and the culture of millet available for third grades; the emphasis on the world of Hannibal in sixth grade; the contrast between the kingdoms of Songhai, Mali and Timbuktu and the European Dark Ages in seventh, just to name a few. In high school, the scope becomes even wider. What really is important however is that each teacher take the openness of the Waldorf curriculum as an incentive towards individual social as well as academic responsibility. We must in our own small ways shine through the sleepy clouds of ignorance and ambivalence. Through an inner redemption of Cain, we not only become "our brother's keeper," but a beacon of hope for all those who would go forward into freedom.

ENDNOTES

1   Carl Stegmann, *The Other America* (Privately published, 1976).
2   L.F.C. Mees, "The White and Black Races," *The Golden Blade*, 1974.
3   Langston Hughes and Arna Bontemps, *The Book of Negro Folklore*, Dodd & Mead, 1958.
4   Ibid.
5   Aha Jablow, *The Intimate folklore of Africa*, Horizon Press, 1961.
6   Joyce Cooper Arkhurst, *More Adventures of Spider*, Scholastic Bookservices, 1972.
7   Harold Courlander, *A Treasury of Afro-American Folklore*, New York: Crown Publishing, 1976.
8   Joel Chandler Harris, *Uncle Remus, His Songs and Sayings*, New York: Appletton, 1880.
9   Rudolf Steiner, "Dialect and the Written Language," *The Renewal of Education*, Steiner Schools Fellowship Pub., U.K.
10   Eugene B. Redmond, *Drumvoices: A Critical History*, New York: Doubleday, 1976.
11. Roark Bradford, *John Henry*, New York: Harpers, 1931.

Additional References

Freire, Paulo, *Education: The Practice of Freedom*, London: Writers & Readers Pub. Co-op, 1976.

Hale-Benson, Janice E., *Black Children: Their Roots, Culture, and Learning Styles*, Johns Baltimore: Hopkins U. Press, 1986.

Haskins, Jim and Hugh F. Butts, *The Psychology of Black Language*, New York: Barnes & Noble, 1973.

Kunjufu, Jawanza, *A Talk with Jawanza* (Critical Issues in Educating African-American Youth), Chicago: African-American Images, 1989.

_______, *Developing Positive Self-images and Discipline in Black Children*, Chicago: African-American Images, 1984.

Mbiti, John S., *African Religions and Philosophies*, New York: Anchor-Doubleday, 1970.

Simonson, Rick and Scott Walker, Eds., *Greywolf Annual No. 5, Multi Cultural Literacy*, St. Paul, MN: Greywolf Press, 1988.

Thompson, Robert Farris, *Flash of the Spirit: African & Afro-American Art and Philosophy*, New York: Vintage Books, 1984.

Africa, my Africa,
Africa of proud warriors in the ancestral savannahs,
Africa my grandmother sings of
Beside her distant river,
I have never seen you
But my gaze is full of your blood,
Your black blood spilt over the fields,
The blood of your sweat,
The sweat of your toil,
The toil of slavery,
The slavery of your children.

Africa, tell me, Africa,
Are you the back that bends,
Lies down under the weight of humbleness?
The trembling back striped red
That says yes to the sjambok on the roads at noon?

Solemnly a voice answers me:
"Impetuous child, that young and sturdy tree,
That tree that grows
There splendidly,
Alone among white and faded flowers
Is Africa, your Africa.
It puts forth new shoots,
With patience and stubbornness puts forth new shoots.
Slowly its fruits grow to have
The bitter taste of liberty."

– David Diop, Senegal

Multiculturalism – A Controversial Issue

Betty Staley, Sacramento Waldorf School, CA

Multicultural education has become an emotional, political issue in educational circles, affecting elementary, high school, and university education. The concern for equal coverage in curriculum has now been taken up by ethnic groups in the country, making demands in curriculum meetings, in publishing houses, and in parent meetings.

What does it mean to say a curriculum should be multicultural? That studies such as literature, art, history and geography should teach not just about the West, but also include contributions from places such as Africa, Asia, Latin America, and so on; that specific courses focus on particular cultures so students can gain a deeper sense of appreciation of these cultures; that the school include an awareness of the multiplicity of cultures and reflect this in the celebrations and customs experienced by the children.

The debate is not a matter of inclusion, but of how much. How much should white culture be emphasized in the history of the Western world and specifically of the United States? How much should non-white cultures be represented? How appropriate or inappropriate is the issue of race in education? Should history be a smorgasbord of cultures or should students be primarily taught a development of Western ideas and culture? Is it either/or, or both? There is a limited amount of time in which to teach and teachers need to have priorities. It is the pressure of these choices that is causing tension in educational establishments all over the nation. In addition to the choices, it is the various viewpoints surrounding historical events that are now being looked at differently.

For example, for generations Columbus Day has been celebrated in a joyful manner in the United States. Columbus has been heralded as the bringer of a new era when he "discovered" the Americas. So it has usually been seen from the point of view of Europeans expanding out of Europe to the Americas. While the 500th anniversary of Columbus' discoveries may be met with joy in one part of the world, it is a time of mourning in another. From the point of view of the Native Americans (North and South) and the Africans, enslaved by Columbus and his followers, his voyages set the foundation for colonialism and a long tradition of exploitation. In this light, can one continue to teach the children a one-sided simplistic picture of Christopher Columbus "sailing the ocean blue"?

Other issues are at stake besides how many courses are taught, what ethnic groups are covered, and how holidays are celebrated. We are being asked to rethink the subject: What is America really?

Review of the Controversy

In New York the debate over multiculturalism has been particularly strong. State Education Commissioner Thomas Sobol set up a panel to suggest guidelines for giving greater recognition to the role of non-white cultures in America. The committee submitted a 97-page report titled "One Nation, Many Peoples: A Declaration of Cultural Interdependence."

Joseph Berger covered the outcome of this report in the *New York Times* (June 21,1991) and stated,

> The battle over the New York State social studies
> curriculum is fundamentally a battle over the idea of
> America. Is the United States a land where immigrants
> and minorities mute their distinct traditions and
> histories to adopt a common, if amorphous, culture?
> Or is it a land where ethnicity should be celebrated over
> and above any shared heritage?…
>
> In some ways, the battle is as old as immigration
> to these shores. Irish, Italian and Jewish youngsters
> endlessly tangle with stubborn parents who want them
> to cling to the customs and faiths they had brought from
> the old country. The more ethnocentric scholars on the
> committee could well identify with the peddlers and
> shoemakers who doggedly fought off assimilation.
>
> The peddlers and shoemakers, however, seldom
> demanded that their cultures be taught in the school
> curriculum. They believed that such instruction was
> a responsibility of family, community or houses of
> worship.
>
> But as the number of Black, Hispanic, Asian and
> American Indian New Yorkers has grown to make up

31 percent of the state's population, many people from these minorities have been increasingly demanding that social studies include their cultures. (p. 1)

The report calls for teachers to change the way they present history.

More than anything, the 24-member panel appears to underscore the idea that even the youngest of students should be taught to view history in a critical manner and to understand that there can be many ways of understanding historical events. Some educators have criticized this approach as distorting history by suggesting that all interpretations are equally valid, and some teachers said today that they were at a loss to understand how young pupils could be helped to make sense of so much deeply conflicting information. (Sam Howe Verhovek, *New York Times*, June 21,1991, p. 4.)

The committee itself was divided on certain issues. Two members of the committee wrote a dissent which was attached to the main report. One of these members objected that the committee was glorifying Africa, India, and other parts of the world by stressing the great loss of lives, torture, and eradication of traditional culture. He said there was much cruelty in these cultures as well—slavery, polygamy, subjection of women, footbinding and clitorectomies. According to historian Arthur M. Schlesinger, the report "plays up the crimes and plays down the ideals" of European explorers and influences. They contend that the report distorts American society." Three members of the committee wrote a rebuttal of the dissent, and they strongly endorsed the report. They said, "The report balances diversity and commonality in ways that benefit all our people, not some at the expense of others."

Some excerpts from the social studies report, "One Nation, Many Peoples: A Declaration of Cultural Interdependency" follow.

"The United States is a microcosm of humanity today. No other country in the world is peopled by a greater variety of races, nationalities and ethnic groups. But although the United States has been a great asylum for diverse peoples, it has not always been a great refuge for diverse cultures. The country has opened its doors to a multitude of nationalities, but often their cultures have not been encouraged to survive or, at best, have been kept marginal to the mainstream.

"Since the 1960s, however, a profound reorientation of the self-image of Americans has been under way. Before this time the dominant model of the typical American has been conditioned primarily by the need to shape a unified nation out of a variety of contrasting and often conflicting European immigrant communities. But following the struggles for civil rights, the unprecedented increase in non-European immigration over the last two decades and the increasing recognition of the nation's indigenous heritage, there has been a fundamental change in the image of what a resident of the United States is.

"With this change, which necessarily highlights the racial and ethnic pluralism of the nation, previous ideals of assimilation to an Anglo-American model have been put in question and are now slowly and sometimes painfully being set aside. Many people in the United States today are no longer comfortable with the requirement, common in the past, that they shed their specific cultural differences in order to be considered American. Instead … many in the United States from European and non-European backgrounds have been encouraging a more tolerant, inclusive and realistic vision of American identity than any that has existed in the past.

"Two centuries after this country's founders issued a Declaration of Independence … the time has come to recognize cultural interdependence. We propose the principle of respect for diverse cultures is critical to our nation, and we affirm that a right to cultural diversity exists. We believe that the schoolroom is one of the places where this cultural interdependence must be reflected…

"Multicultural education is often viewed as divisive and even as destructive to the values which hold us together as Americans. But national unity does not require that we eliminate the very diversity that is the source of our uniqueness… If the United States is to continue to prosper in the 21st century, then all of its citizens, whatever their race or ethnicity, must believe that they and their ancestors have shared in the building of the country and have a stake in its success…

"To improve teaching and learning in the social studies, it will not suffice to change the listing of content and topics to be taught, nor to change the emphasis on history or any other field.

The perceived goal itself must change, for it has become the teaching of large and ever-increasing amounts of information without adequate organizing and supporting frameworks." (p. 4)

The committee realized that trying to list the accomplishments of each group would lead to encyclopedic learning and, even if possible timewise, would not be pedagogically sound. Thus they recommended

> that the approach to the social studies, kindergarten through 12, shift the emphasis from the mastery of information to the development of fundamental tools, concepts and intellectual processes that make people learners who can approach knowledge in a variety of ways and struggle with the contradictions.

Another part of the committee's report was to make teachers more aware that the use of terms such as "races" of people is not appropriate. "Students need to see race as a cultural phenomenon, not a physical description, and need to be able to examine history and how it is used." The term Oriental should be replaced with Asian, Middle East with Southwest Asia and North Africa, slaves with enslaved persons and minorities with "part of the world's majorities."

Some of the committee members expressed concern that so much focus on ethnic groups would heighten an awareness of the differences and possibly encourage the kinds of problems seen today in the republics of the Soviet Union, Canada and Yugoslavia, instead of supporting a common culture. Dr. Kenneth T. Jackson, one of the dissenters, said,

The report has little to say about the things that hold Americans together, like its democratic ideals, however imperfectly observed. History has given Americans a culture that is mainly rooted in Britain but that has been greatly transformed by later tides of immigration. And this, for good or bad, has become the American culture that people aspire to. The people of the United States will recognize, even if this committee does not, that every viable nation has to have a common culture to survive in peace. (p. 4)

Commissioner Sobol hoped a middle ground can be found in the curriculum between a sharing of America's values and an appreciation of its diversity.

Another very active discussion of this question took place when all California school districts but one (Oakland) approved a new Houghton Mifflin Social Studies series. John Leo reported in the *U.S. News & World Report*,

Here is the best news in years on the multicultural front: After a year or two of amazing tribal tumult, California has picked a series of fair and accurate social studies textbooks acceptable in urban and suburban schools alike… All is not peaceful yet. There is still some ethnic grumbling. But California clearly has turned a corner and is pointing the way out of the multicultural mess for school systems in other states. Significantly, this has happened in a state where white children are a minority in public schools and 4 or 5 of every 28 pupils currently speak little or no English.

The key to California's success came not from trying to soothe the feelings of every group, but by asking the question: "What will our children have to know to live in a multicultural world and carry on the American experiment?"

Leo reflects on the different approaches used by New York and California. New York, he claims, made a mistake by including people with polarized views on the panel; California worked with consensus-building with people of all races who were trying to find commonality. The California approach, in trying to set guidelines for the publishers, stressed historical accuracy, civic values and the experience of people from the many ethnic and religious backgrounds that live in the state.

California State Commissioner of Education, Bill Honig, acknowledged the difficulties, but he said, "If you cave in the first time you hear somebody shout 'racist!' you'll never get anything done. If you stand up and say, 'This is right and we're going to do it,' you'll get 95 percent of the people behind you." Though black radicals got most of the ink at hearings, Honig said, "We had black scholars get up and say 'I've been waiting all my life for this book.'" (p. 14)

Having examined the series, Leo considers the books "scrupulously fair to everyone from Black Elk to Columbus. Using anecdotes, biography and social history, the two volumes on America weave together the tales of each group into a credible and highly readable story of America in motion… Religions, ethics and the problems of running a democracy are all taught…

There is emphasis on trends, ideas, pastimes, dress and the lives of ordinary folk. The sins and successes of America are all there. The problem of 'the one and the many' that poisons discussions of multicultural matters has somehow been solved: Individuals, tribes, nation and civic values are all stressed." (p. 14)

I recommend teachers order several of the Houghton Mifflin series to see what a well-balanced approach includes. The teacher can then use these books as a guide to researching materials.

Newsweek, September 23, 1991, devoted several articles to the question of Afrocentrism and multiculturalism. The two sides of Afrocentrism are examined—paying tribute to all the ethnic groups whose history has been neglected in American education and as a way of redressing the balance between blacks and whites. Yet Jerry Adler (and staff) raise the question: "Why should the 'greatest achievements of humankind' belong to either whites or blacks? Are they not by definition universal?"

What we are experiencing more than an educational issue is a political issue. Each group is seeking its own identity outside the mainstream or common identity. It sees the mainstream as its enemy or at the very least its rival. As teachers we walk a fine line between trying to be fair and inclusive, paying tribute to the various cultures without holding one above the other, and at the same time, examining ourselves for biases.

Two black scholars look at the issue from different sides. One of them, Molefi Kete Asante, Chairman of the Department of African-American Studies at Temple University and the author of *Afrocentricity,* says, "In its practical implications, Afrocentricity aims to locate African-American children in the center of the information being presented in classrooms across the nation. Most African-American children sit in classrooms, yet are outside the information being discussed. The white child sits in the middle of the information, whether it is literature, history, politics or art. The task of the Afrocentric curriculum is finding patterns in African-American history and culture that help the teacher place the child in the middle of an intellectual experience. This is not an idea to replace all things European, but to expand the dialogue to include African-American information. An Afrocentric curriculum covers kindergarten through 12th grade in every subject area. It can then be infused into an academic program cleansed of pejoratives like Bushmen and wild Indian in order to have a truly multicultural curriculum."

Waldorf Education

How does the Waldorf curriculum relate to this? Following is a guideline to the various grade levels and the various cultural components. The class teachers can use their creativity to incorporate and expand on the examples below.

Literature is reflected in the Waldorf curriculum through fairy tales, fables, stories of holy (saintly) people, legends, myths, biographies, historical and fictional novels and essays. In all these areas of study, it is expected that the teacher will choose examples from many different cultures in the world.

Let us look at fairy tales which are the focus of the first grade. "Household tales," as they were originally called when the Brothers Grimm collected them in Germany, may be a more appropriate name than "fairy tales." The images in these tales are meant to be lived into in the home. They are an education of archetypes, values and behavior. It is very interesting to see how similar images are expressed in different cultures. For example, the story of "The Daughter Who Would Be Mended" from the Hausa people in West Africa follows the same pattern as "Mother Holle" from the Grimms' tales and could be used in first grade.

In the second grade, fables are a major source for literature. Here animals represent specific human characteristics such as greed, slyness, pride, cleverness. Trickster tales abound in Native American tales, the Anansi Spider tales of West Africa, the Mantis tales of the San people (previously known as the Bushmen), the Uncle Remus stories of the American South, as well as the Aesop fables (which have their origin in Africa), and these can be easily included in the second grade. The stories of the great holy figures, the saints, represent figures in human history who have overcome their lower nature (represented in the fables) and have developed higher qualities such as patience, love, oneness with the animal world and with the world of nature.

In the third grade the blocks on farming, clothing, food, and building lend themselves to examples from many different cultures. How different to farm in a forested area than in a desert area! The problems of water, crop rotation, and harvesting are different. The kinds of animals used are different. How different to build houses in various parts of the world—a thatched hut, a mud brick compound, a house on stilts, an ice igloo, a hogan, a brick apartment house, a stucco house, a wood house in the mountains, and so on! How exciting to teach about the foods of the world—just studying the grains takes us to so many different cultures: rice, rye, wheat, barley, millet, maize (corn). The clothing study also affords rich opportunities to learn how people dress in different parts of the world: to learn to hand-spin and weave a simple object, to see people weaving beautiful fabrics of traditional patterns and colors, to invite people to dress in their native costume for the children.

Local history and geography are explored in the fourth grade. Here is an obvious place to include the cultures of people who explored, settled, and currently make up the city and state. With the expanding variety of immigrants making the United States their home, this block of study can be rich in substance. Throughout the fourth grade, this theme can be a motif, expressing itself in art, history, literature, games, dances, food and clothing. Guest speakers can be invited to share their cultures and discuss how they are becoming part of the local community.

In fifth grade the geography expands to the country. Extending the fourth grade study from the state to the country and continent provides wonderful possibilities to include the geography of the different regions and the people who live there. For example, this is a time for studying the cultures of the Southwest, the people who live there, the landscape, the homes, the agriculture, and the crafts. This can be contrasted with the region of the Northeast, the Northwest with the Southeast, and the central heartland of the country with its river basins, its agriculture, people, etc. Then there is the study of Mexico and Canada, both geographically and culturally. The study of animals can expand to include animals that live in different parts of the world.

The fifth grade history curriculum includes the study of Asia, the Middle East, Africa, and Europe. This includes the great poetry of the Bhagavad Gita and the Vedas, the life of Gotama Buddha, the development of society in India, the teachings of Zarathustra in the kingdoms of Persia (present-day Iran) through the Zend Avesta, the culture that developed in Mesopotamia in the land between the Tigris and Euphrates Rivers (modern Iraq), the ancient kingdom of Egypt as a window into Africa, and the culture of Greece.

The study of botany affords an opportunity to look at the plant life of different places on the earth. What is life like in a forested area, a grassland, the desert, the mountains, the tundra, and so on?

In the sixth grade, Western history develops from Greece to Rome and the Middle Ages. In geography the continents of South America and Africa can be studied, including the land forms, the people who live there, their history and cultures. (I find it particularly valuable to study the geography of South America and Africa before the Renaissance block so the students have an appreciation for the land and culture before the explorations. This can be done in late sixth grade or early seventh grade.) Historically, the teacher can compare the Middle Ages in Europe with the Middle Ages in West Africa at the universities of Timbuktu and Ghana, and the trade from Europe to the Holy Land with the trade across the Sahara. Geography and history are interwoven, with geography connecting the children to the body of the earth and the historical events to the stream of time and cultures.

In seventh and eighth grades, individual countries are studied including the physical conditions, cultural life, economic life, and political life. The students could study Asia and Europe, with Russia bridging the two. One of the key issues in the New York Social Studies report is that of viewing Western migration from a Native American perspective (as well as from the migrants' view). This is very compatible with the Waldorf approach to show the students the polarities in history—two people or cultures which hold different viewpoints of the issue.

Eighth grade geography includes the study of the weather systems and water systems of the world and of economic geography—the whole world of raw materials and production, how products of one region are shared with another. The picture of the interdependence of the world is a central image. Other continents are studied, perhaps Australia and New Zealand or one of the continents I mentioned earlier, so that the children are immersed in the land and cultures of all the major peoples of the world.

In the high school these studies are taken again from a more intellectual viewpoint. In the ninth grade, in history through art, students can become conscious of the universality of art and its relation to the spiritual and practical life. This is shown in the sculpture, painting, and architecture of Asia, Africa, Europe, and pre-Columbian art in the Americas. These studies continue in the upper grades, including the influence of Asian art on the West, for example, with the French Impressionists, and of the African mask on Picasso and thus on modern art.

In 10th, 11th, and 12th grade history blocks, the students study modern world history; American history; ancient history including many different cultures of the world; European history: Greek, Roman, Medieval, Renaissance; and the histories of Asia, Africa, and Latin America. This tapestry of the history of peoples climaxes with the broad overview of the study of the history of ideas, philosophy and psychology.

Literature is studied in English classes and also in connection with history and geography. The teacher looks for opportunities to highlight the importance of the many peoples of the earth, their contributions to human life, and how they have been treated by the dominant culture—whether it be the development of blood plasma by the African-American Dr. Charles Drew or the treatment of the Japanese during World War II in *Farewell to Manzanar*. The biographies of great figures are included in history, science, and English classes.

In teaching American history, the issues central to the New York State task force are relevant: What is America? Is there more to the American dream than economic opportunity? What is the "other" America that speaks to the idealism behind the "noble experiment"? Is America a melting pot? Is America a collection of ethnic communities, or is there an overriding commonality that is "American" which makes the ethnic groups different than they are in their native lands? In his essay "The American

Scholar," 19th century philosopher Ralph Waldo Emerson called upon us to "deliver the postponed expectations of the world in something better than the exertions of mechanical skill."

As Waldorf teachers we are called upon to wrestle with these questions. The excitement of being a Waldorf teacher is that we have an education rooted in the spiritual view of the human being. Each human being is unique and valuable, and each culture contributes to the human expression on earth. The challenge is to each one of us individually to be awake and alert, not to fall back on old forms and unconsciously carry on old ways of looking at people, but to be true to our calling and appreciate the way each human being can be an expression of truth, goodness, and beauty.

Tassili Frescoes

Thoughts on Teaching a Block on Africa

Susan Cook, San Francisco Waldorf School

For an eighth grade block I treated Africa in terms of
a.   sub-Saharan Africa, and
b.   northern Africa as part of the Arab world/Middle East.

Time was too short and I tried to cram too much into the three-week block of geography that included Africa, the Middle East, Asia, and the Ocean World. The general outline of the section on Africa was:

I.   The geographical features

II.   Main climate regions: general rainfall, temperature pattern, desert, mountains, Mediterranean

III. People of the past and elements of culture that came from them: ancient tribes, trade empires, slave empires, colonialism, independence

IV. Way of life: nomads, hunters, farmers, city-dwellers, crops, families, clans, tribes

V.   Religion: West Africans, Bantus, Pygmies, Europeans, Asians, Hamites

There are two highlights that stand out in hindsight:

1. reading *Cry of the Kalahari* by Mark and Delia Owens. Not much about the people of the region but powerful impressions of the land and wildlife.

2. a visit from Waldorf teacher Monica Marshall and her slides from South Africa.

Following is one example of a student's work:

What I Thought Was Most Interesting about *The Cry of the Kalahari*

The Cry of the Kalahari is a true story of an American couple who lived and did research in the Kalahari Desert. In the dry season in the Kalahari, the wildebeest herds migrated north to where the water was. As these thousands of animals crossed through the Kalahari Game Reserve, the lions and other carnivores' stomachs soon became satisfied after months of barely eating anything. The rest of the wildebeest (that aren't devoured by lions) continued on their exhausting journey north.

The wildebeests were starting to smell water as they almost neared the water hole, which caused them to move with more enthusiasm. As they continued, slowly getting weaker for lack of water, they came upon a tall fence. This was curious to them, but as they realized that they could not pass this fence, they suddenly grew even more exhausted and many stopped to rest—never to wake again.

The other wildebeest turned and walked along the fence, traveling further away from their destiny, but they had no other choice. Finally they reached an ending to the fence and started traveling directly towards the water. The sun grew hotter and the scent of water grew stronger. Some wildebeests made it to the waterhole but some didn't, as there were poachers who killed these animals and also some died of exhaustion. Mark and Delia observed all of this and fought and are still fighting against poaching in this area.

Recommendations from Class Teachers

I strongly recommend *Indaba My Children* by Vusamazulu Credo Mutwa. (After his woman was killed at Sharpeville, he decided to forsake the secrecy under which he was bound as a witch doctor and tell the story of his people.) This book is a wonderful and unique chronicle of tribal lore and culture. Out of our study of geography in the seventh grade where we were also learning the legends and stories of the African tribes, we studied a tribe that gave a specific task to all the children at the age of thirteen when they were going through an initiation to pass through the outer gate of childhood.

The African children were required to write poems in a specific style as exemplified below. As a rite of passage for my seventh grade class, I gave them this same exercise in their English class. The following are some of the many poems which the class wrote:

Young man you are:
a light in the dark night,
a reflection in a deep pool,
a wolf among sheep,
a song that hasn't been sung,
a never ending book.

Young woman you are:
a birch tree swaying in the wind,
a moonbeam shining on a lake,
a fire that never burns out,
a grain of sand on the beach,
an apple that ripens in the sun.

Young woman you are:
a caterpillar that becomes a butterfly,
a hornet that has a piercing sting,
a waterfall which keeps on flowing,
a leaf that never falls to the ground.

Young man you are:
a bird that flies into a hail storm,
an alligator being pulled out of the mud,
a wall going up beyond the clouds in the sky,
an ant crawling into a nest of bees,
a helpless animal in a pit of quicksand.

This book is available from Rudolf Steiner College Bookstore,
9200 Fair Oaks Blvd., Fair Oaks, CA 95628.

– DAVID MITCHELL, Pine Hill Waldorf School, NH

Russell Meek from the San Francisco Waldorf School recommends *Kilimanjaro: A Photographic Journey to the Roof of Africa* for literature. He says it has wonderful prose and pictures, and is extremely informative and up-to-date.

Manette Teitelbaum from the Marin Waldorf School recommends World Music Press, publisher of multicultural music publications for teachers. They also carry some tapes, records, and books that are hard to find and are useful.

Dmitri Laury

High School Curriculum on Africa

Jim Staley, Sacramento Waldorf School, CA

Experiences Teaching the Africa Block

This course has been taught in our school for over ten years, first by Keith Jefferson, then by me. The content of the course has been shaped by the following:

1. A judgment on my part that it was far more urgent to provide the youngsters with a solid foundation of geography and history than to deal with the specific details and complexities of contemporary Africa. The contemporary situation is always in the room with us and it gets referred to over and over, but we do not attempt to master the details of social, political, economic problems.

2. The fact that the vast majority of African-Americans have their roots in Western Africa.

3. The judgment that West African history provides the most dramatic and powerful antidotes to the traditional American stereotypes about Africa and African people.

4. The fact that I personally know much more about West Africa and have a stronger interest in West Africa than in other areas of the continent. Consequently, we now teach a three-week course. In the first week we introduce the students to African

geography (with considerable mapwork) and to the ancient history of Africa, including the distribution of the various races native to Africa. In the second week, we focus on the Sudanic and forest kingdoms of West Africa, including the Islamization of the Sahel, the trans-Saharan trade, and a superficial inventory of the other pre-colonial cultures elsewhere. In the third week, we deal with the changes brought by European influences, especially the slave trade and then the 1885–1965 colonial era and the decolonization during the 1950s and 60s. In past years, I also have done a lot with apartheid, but I cut that back sharply this year on the assumption that this issue will be moving out of the center of U.S.-African issues. I also try to alert the students to the social, economic, and political issues which are common to African countries and which are even generic to the Third World.

This latter focus increases and decreases a lot from class to class. The students often say that the course was one of their high school favorites. There often is a strong desire to visit Africa after the course is over, and a handful of students have actually done so. A larger handful have made a point of taking college courses on Africa. I feel that the course provides the youngsters with some solid ground to stand on in developing an attitude of respect toward Africa and Africans in an environment which otherwise offers very little basis for such respect.

In recent years, I have made increasing use of African music, which provides a great bridge into the culture for our students. It also confronts them with the cultural diversity of Africa itself when they discover how different the music is from place to place.

Resources

Mapwork is an important element in this course, and we have a huge and excellent map of Africa which hangs front-and-center throughout the course. This was an expensive investment for the school, but I believe it is invaluable. African novels are readily available in paperback, and poetry somewhat available. Ditto for books of folk tales and surveys of handicrafts and other artworks. Information on history, religion, economics, art, archeology, etc., is available in far more detail than we can ever use in a survey course, but it is usually packaged in college-level and professional academic formats, which means that the secondary teacher must do a lot of digesting and reforming of the material to prepare it for classroom use. I haven't even made a dent in what's available, partly because it's so formidable.

Waldorf teachers want to present living images to their classes, but the kind of lively, colorful biographical information which is so abundantly available for some cultures is extremely scarce for Africa. Ancient personages are only known to us— if at all—through very one-dimensional accounts, and modern figures are often heads of state whose biographies are also very wooden and uncritical, lacking the kind of texture and color which so much helps a lesson to live. We are really hampered by the fact that so much of African culture has been and still is transmitted by oral tradition.

Multiculturalism and Music

Barbara Francis, Rudolf Steiner School, NY

This year our high school has introduced a course on African drums as part of our music program. Three periods a week immediately following the break after main lesson, all students are taken through courses in recorder, vocal music, chamber music, bottle band and performance on African drums. These courses run concurrently in blocks of time for various groups of mixed classes. This particular course arises through the good auspices of our high school biology teacher, Rick Shrum (a WASP), who has learned the art with his (Jewish) wife as a recreational activity. This is real multiculturalism, and the students love it!

As part of the high school music program, I taught the song "Amazing Grace" by giving a historical sketch of its origins and its subsequent evolution among different peoples as part of their culture. PBS produced an extraordinary documentary on this theme in December 1990, and I was inspired by the story and the particular quality of the presentation depicting the amazing effect it has had on people's lives, particularly in the Afro-American community.

The song was written by John Newton (1725–1807), an Englishman who was a callous slave-trader with no particular ethical or spiritual impulses worthy of note. One day, up on the ship's deck in the middle of the ocean, *a propos* of nothing in particular, he suddenly had a transforming experience. He was silently moved by something beyond himself that wakened his whole sensibility in a startlingly new way—and which changed his life completely. As a result of this invisible event in his life, he wrote this song in amazement and gratitude for the transforming power of this moment. He gave up his former profession, started speaking out against the slave trade, and became a clergyman in order to give his life to these new spiritual and ethical perceptions.

The song has since rolled 'round the world and has been picked up with unusual fervor by the descendants of Newton's original cargo, the Afro-American community. Opera star Jessye Norman has become a magnificent artistic interpreter and eloquent spokeswoman for the power of this particular song in its ability to change people's lives. It was picked up by the musicians in the 60s and became universally favored during the civil rights efforts of that era. It is a significant fact that the Afro-American communities as well as the native African communities have these wonderfully strong musical inclinations and traditions which are still active to a great extent today. Singing together provides meaningful social glue, and the experience of these particular musical traditions can be spell-binding in the extent to which the music is a natural part of daily life and is all-inclusive—male and female, young and old.

We, in the WASP communities of the Northeast, have no similar binding force in the musical sphere except for the waning tradition of singing Christmas carols once a year. Our communities, by contrast, have become noticeably impoverished in recent years as we have gradually become exclusive listeners rather than active participants.

Multiculturalism and Literature

Barbara Francis, Rudolf Steiner School, NY

In the winter of 1989–90, during a study of Alan Paton's *Cry the Beloved Country*, I assigned some supplementary reading to my students on the life of Nelson Mandela. Before we finished reading the book, we were astonished and delighted when his release suddenly came about. Coming together with the echoes ringing in our ears from Paton's words, this event inspired us to put together an assembly presentation based on the students' own writing about Mandela interspersed with choral speech out of Paton's book.

Our astonishment and joy increased yet again shortly thereafter when Mandela arrived in our own town, setting off a wave of euphoria throughout the city. The wonderful response was inspired by tremendous hero-worship of someone who had achieved his freedom through self-mastery. There was a new sense of brotherhood across racial lines which was unique among heroes' welcomes in all the years past. Following are a few extracts from our assembly presentation:

There is a time of sadness and a time of fear. There is a time of decline, a time of victory, and above all a time of joy. The time comes in everyone's life. During the past few weeks, the tenth grade has been reading Alan Paton's *Cry the Beloved Country*. During this time, Nelson Mandela was released from his South

African prison cell after twenty-seven years of imprisonment. South Africa's time of victory has come, and we would like to share some of their pain, some of their joy and some of their victory with you by reading some passages from *Cry the Beloved Country*, as well as some excerpts honoring Mandela written by the sophomore class.

Cry, the beloved country, for the unborn child that is the inheritor of our fear. Let him not love the earth too deeply. Let him not laugh too gladly when the water runs through his fingers, nor stand too silent when the setting sun makes red the veld with fire. Let him not be too moved when the birds of his land are singing, nor give too much of his heart to a mountain or a valley. For fear will rob him of all if he gives too much. (Paton)

Nelson Mandela was born in 1916 in South Africa in a small village near a river. When he was a child, he used to listen to the old men's stories about the great life in their native land as it was before the white people came to be rulers. From his early days he felt the wonder and magnificence of all those hills, rivers, fertile lands, forests—his heritage. He loved it because all men born on that land cannot help but feel the closest connection with their country's nature.

This land is a beautiful land: his land and the land of his people. This land provided him with the memories that helped him to survive his long years in prison. Vivid recollections were dear to him: names and landscapes and maybe the village itself where he was born. He lived in prison for twenty-seven years, and his imaginative pictures of the land sustained him. His life in jail didn't break him down. He is still full of energy. He knows what he wants. He knows how to bring happiness to his people, and he will do it! His land will help him. (This was written by a Refusenik Jew who emigrated from Leningrad to Brooklyn under the previous regime only six months before.)

*And now for all the people of Africa, the beloved country. Nkosi Sikelel iAfrika, God save Africa. But he would not see that salvation. It lay afar off, because men were afraid of it. Because, to tell the truth, they were afraid of him. And what was there evil in their desires, in their hunger? That men should walk upright in the land where they were born and be free to use the fruits of the earth, what was there evil in it? Yet men were afraid, with a fear that was deep, deep in the heart, a fear so deep that they hid their kindness, or brought it out with fierceness and anger, and hid it behind fierce and frowning eyes. They were afraid because they were so few. And such fear could not be cast out, but by love ...
I have one great fear in my heart that one day when they turn to loving, they will find we are turned to hating. (Paton)*

As the rooster sang and the day dawned in the one dark corner of a sun-filled hut, a shadow was cast on the wall; a baby's cry sounded: a great man was born: Nelson Mandela, prince of his small thatch-roofed town. A proud leader this small child would one day become. Through hardships and blessed times, out of the little boy, an amazing young man was emerging: an activist who believed in a dream, a man who was loved by all his people, a man who was feared by his government, a mysterious man too proud to back away from the heavy burden of leadership, a wonderful man who was crowned in a jail cell, a man who didn't let go, who clung to his rights. Offers were made, business deals; they tried to persuade him to compromise his integrity; now an old man who gripped the silver-colored iron bars, a man who was prepared to die for his beloved country, a man who last month was let go, a man who was finally free. He didn't need a battle. He just made them see. (A student from New Jersey)

Who indeed knows the secret of the earthly pilgrimage? Who knows for what we live, and struggle, and die? Who knows what keeps us living and struggling, while all things break about us? Who knows why the warm flesh of a child is such comfort, when one's own child is lost and cannot be recovered? Wise men write many books, in words too hard to understand. But this, the purpose of our lives, the end of all our struggle, is beyond all human wisdom. Oh God, my God, do not Thou forsake me. Yea, though I walk through the valley of the shadow of death, I shall fear no evil, if Thou art with me... (Paton)

Life is a question. There is always a question and doubt in every living soul. Individuals do not seem to be bonded to one another, although in some way or other we are. A common theme in every individual's life is the desire for freedom. Some people live just to die, and others live for what they strive for. Some care and others don't. Nelson Mandela is an individual with a strong soul. He lives for others. He gave up the most beautiful years of his life for the freedom of his own people. (A student from Puerto Rico)

Therefore I shall devote myself, my time, my energy, my talents, to the service of South Africa. I shall no longer ask myself

*if this or that is expedient, but only if it is right. I shall do this,
not because I am noble or unselfish, but because life slips away,
and because I need for the rest of my journey a star that will
not play false to me, a compass that will not lie. I shall do this,
because I cannot find it in me to do anything else. I am lost when
I balance this against that, I am lost when I ask if this is safe, I am
lost when I ask if men, white men or black men, Englishmen or
Afrikaners, Gentiles or Jews, will approve. Therefore I shall try to
do what is right, and to speak what is true. I do this not because I
am courageous and honest, but because it is the only way to end
the conflict of my deepest soul. I do it because I am no longer able
to aspire to the highest with one part of myself and to deny it with
another. I do not wish to live like that, I would rather die than
live like that. I understand better those who have died for their
convictions, and have not thought it was wonderful or brave or
noble to die. They died rather than live, that was all. Yet it would
not be honest to pretend that it is solely an inverted selfishness
that moves me. I am moved by something that is not my own,
that moves me to do what is right, at whatever cost it may be.*
(Paton)

Nelson Mandela is a man who is held in high esteem, and
that high esteem has been with him since the day of his noble
birth. Nelson Mandela was born into the royal family of the
Timbo Tribe that occupies the Transkei. When Mandela was
growing up, he had a life of tribal splendor, but as he crept into
adulthood, pain and catastrophe tried to strike him down. After
he received his law degree, he decided that he would dedicate
his life to ending apartheid in South Africa. This dedication and

strong will led him into prison for twenty-seven years. While in prison, he remained a prince with princely stature and dignity. His release last month signaled that the prince has returned to lead his people. (A student from Nigeria)

And the east lightened and lightened, till he knew that the time was not far off. And when he expected it, he rose to his feet and took off his hat and laid it down on the earth, and clasped his hands before him. And while he stood there the sun rose in the east.

Yes, it is the dawn that has come … as it has come for a thousand centuries, never failing. But when that dawn will come, or our emancipation, from the fear of bondage and the bondage of fear, why, that is a secret. (Paton)

The Celebration of Kwanzaa

Barbara Francis, Rudolf Steiner School, NY

While the problems and challenges of life in a big city continue to gather momentum, friends and family continue to ask why I have not taken flight to a more harmonious rural or suburban setting. Perhaps one of the chief factors that binds me to the difficult urban setting is the extent to which I am forced to establish a relationship with a wide variety of people who come from such vastly different backgrounds in the ethnic, religious and socio-economic spheres. Social complacency is an impossibility here. Communities are formed out of mutual interest rather than out of common backgrounds; thus an individual belongs to a variety of different communities containing very different types of people according to the particular activity or interest one is pursuing at any one time, as well as the communities through which one passes "face to face" while in transit; the circles overlap.

When I retreat to a rural community in the summer in order to commune with Thoreau's world of nature and restore my soul in quietness, the surrounding communities provide me with experiences of people whose backgrounds are very similar to my own. This was also true of the suburban community where I grew up and where I attended school as a child. But when I return to my big city, I am always stimulated by the necessity to experience these wide encounters—to find the way to recognize the different countenances that the human family wears and the magnitude of variety in the wave beats of the human heart. It is here that I begin to unravel the mystery of my fellow man, and above all, to take a deep interest in the differences.

Around the time of the winter solstice in my neighborhood, we expand our imaginations in our search for appropriate words to use in extending greetings to one another in our numerous encounters: my Italian grocer, the Arab cab driver, the Korean florist and vegetable man, the Indian or Pakistani sandwich-maker in the deli, the Chinese takeout and laundry-man, the Tibetan sellers of books and purveyors of musical instruments, my Eastern European shoemaker, the homeless and down-and-out of every cast and color asking for a handout, my Jewish neighbors issuing from the synagogue around the corner, the Hispanic-Black-White community emerging from their varied activities at the church next door, or the Afro-American families coming away from the Kwanzaa celebrations at the Museum of Natural History. All these people are my near neighbors, within a few blocks of my house. And while the reports of rising crime and violence go out, we continue to greet one another as neighbors in this extraordinary mix of humanity which never fails to touch me deeply.

Teaching in a big city provides a unique opportunity for nurturing this sense of appreciation for the wide variety in the family of man. I have found that in the early grades, one of the best ways to incorporate a better feeling for these varied approaches to life is through the various festival celebrations in the year. This is best done by enlisting the help of those families in the classroom that actually celebrate these different festivals in their homes.

The last time I taught a first grade, I chose Advent as the time to introduce to the children the numbers in their archetypal qualities. In this connection, one family came to help with the Hanukkah celebration as a reflection of the number eight. (This particular kind of help over the years gave me the confidence out of my WASP background to create one on my own for the whole high school in December 1990.)

Two families with ties to Uganda introduced me to the Afro-American celebration of Kwanzaa. This was done in connection with the number seven as reflected in the lighting of seven red, black and green candles on the kbara (similar to a menorah) on the seven nights between December 26 and January 1st. The festival was new to me at the time, but I discovered that the Museum of Natural History, a few blocks from my house, regularly presents Kwanzaa festival events and is an excellent source of study for the novice in this sphere. Since my first celebration in that first grade, the festival has become more well-known and accepted in the city. I learned that this came into being in 1966 through the inspiration of Dr. Maulana Karenga, a civil rights leader, who sought to create a new festival for the future which could serve as a cultural source of brotherhood for the Afro-American community which seeks to establish its own celebration of family, community and culture.

Our classroom provided a wide floor-space as its forum. We covered it with colorful African cloths of yellow, brown, black, burgundy and green. We all sat around the kbara in a wide circle on the floor while the two parents provided some music with drums and singing. Next they shared with us the significance of the candles on the kbara as each candle was lit. The children were given the opportunity to light one of the candles or to hold a hand-written card with the African and English translations of the seven virtues or principles illuminated by each candle: responsibility, creativity, faith, unity, self-determination, purpose, and cooperation in the economic sphere. These can be shared through miniature vignettes of stories or one continuous story bound together by a single character. The kbara was surrounded by a special bowl or dish with fruits of the earth and a special drinking cup, as well as simple gifts for each child, such as a box of raisins beautifully wrapped in yellow.

For the little children, the chance to sit with the use of different colors and a different style of simple music went a long way toward the evocation of a different mood of consciousness and a feeling of appreciation for the different moods that the season can evoke in our town: Advent (for the number four), Hanukkah and Kwanzaa.

Two Representatives of East Africa

Betty Staley, Sacramento Waldorf School, CA

I was privileged to be invited to Jim Staley's 12th grade main lesson in African studies during which two guests addressed the class. The two visitors represented two streams of African culture—one was John Shoka, a professor at California State University, Sacramento; the other was Sajad Janmohamed, a medical doctor and past parent at the Sacramento Waldorf School. The two grew up in Tanzania, but they met in Sacramento and have become good friends. Following are my notes.

John Shoka

John described his childhood in Tanzania. His life took him from tribal culture to African culture to American culture. There are over 500 tribal groups in Africa, 100 plus in Tanzania, each with its own culture and language. John urged that we not make sweeping generalizations about Africa. There are many differences, for example, in the city or country, in religion, and in cultures. Each person lives in three cultures. First, there is the traditional African culture, the indigenous culture which predominates in rural areas. Here we see tribal differences. Second, there is modern culture which is very much influenced by the European. Differences here include whether there is a Protestant or Catholic influence. Third, there is Arab or Islamic culture. Here the Arab and Indian people predominate. So when we speak of African culture, we need to know which level of culture we are referring to. For example, within Dar Es Salaam, you find people on each level. John's father was a tribal chief in Sukumaland, near Lake Victoria. This is the largest tribe in Tanzania, about five million people. Yet it is not mentioned in books. Why? They are not a particularly unique tribe and therefore they don't attract anthropologists. For example, they don't have "strange" markings on their bodies. They are predominantly an agricultural people who grow cotton and corn.

John was born in 1930 in an American Protestant Mission hospital which employs many American doctors. As a young man, his life was quite simple. He did not have access to technology. He played and made his trucks out of corn or millet stalks. He went hunting with arrows made of wire spokes. With his dogs, he hunted deer. There was no electricity. At night, as in most traditional African cultures, people sat around the fire (made from burning cow dung). There the elders told stories and customs—the oral tradition which transmitted the history and culture of the people. Many of these stories told them how to avoid certain things, but in story form. For example, lazy people met tragedy, good people were rewarded. Also they sang tribal songs. John knows close to two hundred tribal songs. Sukuma and Swahili are two of many Bantu languages. Bantu languages are related the way German and English are related. John learned skills by being shown.

Education took place in the village. He went to primary school (grades 1–4), run by the local government. He read and wrote in Swahili, the key language of Tanzania. The local grocery stores were run by an Arab or Indian who spoke Swahili. At home his family spoke their tribal language, Sukuma. He learned Sukuma and Swahili simultaneously. Then he went to a missionary school run by the Dutch. In fifth grade he learned English as a foreign language. By eighth grade he was expected to know enough English to have all his subjects taught in English since this was the language of the British rulers. After he finished 10th grade, he attended public school in Tabora, run by the British. Here he prepared for exams sent from England.

Upon completing school, he went to the capital, Dar Es Salaam, where he worked in broadcasting. In 1989 a large number of African students, especially from Kenya, came to the United States on scholarships negotiated by Kenyan political leader Thomas Mboya. Many of these students were not really ready for college. Some were sent to the South where they confronted racism for the first time. In May 1961, a long article was written about these problems.

John was working in a large diamond mine, trying to Africanize the Civil Service. Because of the problems written about the United States, his Scottish boss warned him not to go to America, but to stay in Tanzania and the British would train him for an important position. At that time, related John, there was very little racism in Britain. His father had been sent to England for nine months in 1956 and reported that he experienced no racism in Britain, although the British in Africa were racist. So John was urged to continue his education in Britain. However, a professor from Berkeley, California, was finding homes in the United States for African students to come and be educated here.

One of John's friends came to California. Soon John received a letter from a family in Ross, near San Raphael, inviting him to come live with them while continuing his studies. This was very exciting. All John knew of the United States was Harry Belafonte and John F. Kennedy. This American program sponsored two charter flights a year to bring African students from Nairobi to the United States. All the student had to do was get a reservation. John made a reservation, but he missed the flight because of a problem with his immigration papers. So he had to pay for his flight. His flight took him by way of London and Scotland to New York. From there he took a Greyhound bus to San Francisco with $70 in his pocket. He arrived with two misconceptions of the United States: Everyone was rich. All whites were racists. At Tabora he had been trained to be a little British gentleman so he would stand out in America.

But Americans had misconceptions about Africans, about their clothing and their food, and that they had elephants in their backyard. But Africa has modern cities. However, if you go outside the city a few miles, you are back to the Middle Ages. Another American misconception is that Africans are anti-white. Most Africans have not even been exposed to whites. Most have not experienced racism. Of course, it is a different situation in South Africa, Kenya, Algeria, Zimbabwe, and Angola where large numbers of white settlers took land away from the Africans and then passed segregation laws. But 80 percent of Africa did not experience this. Therefore these Africans were curious about white people, not angry. They thought white people were like babies.

John began studying, first at the College of Marin, then San Francisco State University. He received a PhD from the University of Washington. This prepared him for his career as a professor of Political Science and International Relations.

Sajad Janmohamed

Sajad Janmohamed's family is one of the many Asian families in East Africa. He reminded us that the history of Africa is the history of invasions and migrations. The Indian Ocean has been a link with India and Arabia, not a barrier. People used the trade winds to come from Asia and Arabia to Africa. In Dar es Salaam, every fourth or fifth person is Asian. Most Indians are traders there. This is not true in the interior of the country.

British rule encouraged Indians to trade along the coast of Africa. With independence came winds of change. Tanzania decided to become a socialist nation. There would be no free trade. This created a conflict, not a racial conflict, but an economic conflict. However, the Indians saw it as racist. This has been difficult as Asians have tried to work this out, but they have had to give up what they gained. Asians are welcome in Tanzania as long as they are willing to work within socialism. Out of the 15 million people in Tanzania, there are about 100,000 Indians. In Dar Es Salaam storekeepers and doctors tend to be Asians or Arabs. In West Africa, the merchants tend to be Lebanese. In Tanzania there was lukewarm apartheid. Indians, Europeans and Africans all went to separate schools. It was when Sajad went to Makerere University in Uganda that he had his first real contact with Africans. A handful of British controlled Africa, and Indians were created as the middlemen, the businessmen and clerks. They were the privileged, while the Africans were the downtrodden. The Governor was appointed by the Queen. He had ultimate power over the people, yet he signed letters, "Your obedient servant." There were no democratic rights.

Sajad's parents were born in Africa. His grandfather had come to Madagascar. Indians had been coming to Africa for a long time. Trade between India and Africa included exchange of African raw materials for Indian spices and textiles. At home Sajad spoke the Indian language and ate Indian food.

After attending medical school, Sajad offered to bring his medical expertise to Uganda, but he was turned down because there was a strong bias against Indians at that time. So he moved to the United States. Currently he practices medicine at Kaiser-Permanente. (I know from other conversations with Sajad Janmohamed that Albert Schweitzer inspired him to become a doctor.)

*　*　*

Sajad and John then spoke of the political changes going on in Tanzania. Tanzania has embarked on a one-party democracy which seems to be working well. It has all the elements of freedom in the constitution. John was there last summer and said it was not repressive, although a few years ago it was very repressive. In some areas, people were forced from their villages and their homes were bulldozed. The socialist government wanted to build new villages. In 1967 there was a declaration to put Tanzania on a socialist path. The government nationalized industries and banks. Eighty per cent of the economy was put in the hands of peasants. The economy was collectivized, and peasants were forced to collectivize more. They were forced out of their villages with their village identity and community and made to live on one common farm. However, most people are disillusioned with one-party democracy. Consequently, there is a lot of searching going on and it seems likely the one-party system will give way to a multiparty system in the near future. Hopefully, this will be done peacefully.

Report from South Africa

Monica Marshall, Mountain Meadow Waldorf School, CA

Three years ago I had the opportunity to appreciate what is really meant when we speak of Waldorf education as a world movement. I spent two summers in South Africa working with the Baobab Center, nurturing the ideals of Waldorf in the Black community.

At that time the Baobab group consisted of five women. Claartje, my connection through the Glenbrook Curative Conferences, has been teaching for over thirty years. She was the founder of the Tobias schools in Holland and had a wealth of experience to share. Truus is a eurythmist with extensive experience working in the U.S. prison system. Maxine, Carol, and Sue are South Africans and bring such diverse talents as a Dornach speech training, Social Development training, and incredible organizational and social skills.

From the moment I arrived, things moved at a non-stop pace. I was amazed at the dedication these women had towards their task to nurture Waldorf education as a community-supported movement that was living and changing to meet the needs of Black South Africa. Non-whites (to use the government's classification), Blacks, Coloreds and Indians have also attended these schools. But there was never a truly non-racial school located in the townships, with a curriculum that answered the needs of that community.

I came to Johannesburg when Baobab Center had already laid the foundation for their working in the townships. They had begun with community activities, because unlike the U.S. where a Waldorf school can flourish without any connection to the surrounding community, nothing survives in the township without community support. First artistic activities were offered to the children. Countless formal and informal meetings took place with residents and social leaders. Workshops were offered through the Greater Soweto Teachers' Association, and teachers who were really interested in Waldorf were trained as the first teachers of a pioneer kindergarten in Alexandra Township.

By the time I arrived in 1988 there was a kindergarten with four classes in Alexandra Township, the plan for a grade school in Alexandra, a craft self-help group located at a home for the elderly, regular teaching visits to state schools in Soweto, and continuous workshops for state teachers from all the townships around Johannesburg. Through the workshops, groups were forming in the different townships to further initiate Waldorf endeavors. In Kwa Zulu a school opened on a biodynamic farm to serve the needs of the children of Zulu farm workers. These teachers were also trained by the Baobab Center.

As soon as I stepped into the township, I felt my heart open to the people. It was wintertime, very cold, and people were huddled over metal drums, burning anything to stay warm. The air was thick with smoke and the smell of burning plastic. The kindergarten was located in a church surrounded by the shacks—some of cement, some of cardboard—of their neighbors. Piles of garbage (no collection in the townships) lay everywhere. Children, dogs, and cows shared the space, the children playing, the dogs and cows foraging. Everyone greeted us with hugs and handshakes. Claartje took me to meet Grace, the "Grandmother of Alexandra" who watched over the site and various other neighbors. People were everywhere. One man lived in half a car right outside the kindergarten outhouses. Women were washing clothes in community sinks, people were selling food, singing, laughing. And everywhere beautiful children were playing, greeting us with big smiles.

My impressions from that initial meeting stayed true for me through my stay. No matter what was happening politically or on the physical plane, the people I met were always filled with their faith in the spiritual world and ready to move forward into the future with hope. Much of my day-to-day work was with women, for they are the childminders (day care providers), and most of the teachers. They also ran many of the community organizations.

I found working in Africa to be very freeing for me as a Waldorf teacher. In the U.S. I made sure I was well prepared for my lessons; my classes worked with the finest materials. Our children are nurtured in an environment that shields them from the demands of our society. In Africa I often came up with lessons on the spur of the moment—both for children and to demonstrate for teachers. We were lucky to have a good supply of used computer paper for the children to draw on. Often there would be violence in the neighborhood around the kindergarten. The man living in his car played his radio very loudly during the day. And still the children came every day—obviously well cared for. And their play was imaginative and peaceful despite the modeling they saw around them.

I quickly settled into a full schedule of activities. Once a week I went with Claartje to a state school in Soweto. The Headmistress at Itacolomeng School was a wonderful woman. Her interactions with the community and her strength in dealing with everyday crises were inspirational. Each week I taught in two or three grades. The sixty or so children in each class were very responsive although most didn't speak English. I usually worked with drama, music and circle activities—all coming out of a dramatic storytelling which the teacher translated also dramatically into whatever the dominant language was in the classroom.

It was a time for the teacher to see new possibilities for learning through movement and the arts, and to reinforce positive discipline styles, for the teachers are encouraged to continue physical discipline. The children were easy to move in such large groups because they were so polite. I found myself delighted when they would become very lively during drama, when the lions roared, the elephants trumpeted or the wind whistled. Form drawing and drawing were also favorite lessons. I found the children to be wonderfully free with colors; rich green cows found places in multi-colored kraals; and I noticed a freer attitude in my own drawing after Africa.

As Baobab trainers, we met once a week to plan weekly workshops for state teachers. Usually two people ran the classes, but sometimes we all shared subjects we were attracted to. The normal group consisted of 20–75 state teachers of young children. We'd meet for four hours on such diverse subjects as "Creative Discipline" or "The Universality of Fairy Tales." One of my favorite workshops was a series Carol and I did on "The Healing Aspects of Child Study." People are very responsive to the spiritual core of Waldorf so even in a beginning workshop, we were free to really delve into the connection between the spiritual world and our work with children. People were often shy and it usually took music and movement to engage the group.

On a personal level I found leading the groups to be a great learning experience. Preparing something from the "inside out" from the spiritual to the physical was very uplifting. I discovered new aspects of Waldorf education and deeper ways of looking at things I already thought I knew. The slow, thoughtful and usually eloquent contributions of people created a mood of true reverence. I am a person of quick and direct responses, so a much-needed quality of patience was given many opportunities to develop.

I should add that people traveled to these workshops from many Johannesburg townships. Travel is not always easy or safe—some spent hours reaching Soweto. By my second summer in Africa, regular attendees from other townships were leading their own groups. Miriam, a Soweto woman, went to Sweden to train. She began a Waldorf kindergarten in Soweto. She trained teachers and began to lead classes with the Baobab center. In Sharpeville a woman had a kindergarten in a garage with eighty children. The social worker who organized the child minders worked regularly with Baobab. Many workshops on creative play and discipline and seasonal festivals were developed for this group.

During the summer of 1988, I worked in the kindergarten classes with their curriculum, but by the next year, Theo had begun a first grade in one of the teacher's garages. As a class teacher myself, I was excited about working with older children. I worked with Theo on basic curriculum, and we all met for faculty meetings. They were always lively, trying to blend two cultures into something meaningful. I took on a lot of specialty classes, sharing games, music, and drama. We all benefited from discussing our sometimes quite different ways of approaching subjects. Lorna, who was to take the next first grade, flew up from Cape Town and we spent two intense days going over curriculum. She has since begun her class with 35 children.

At that time the school was in the center of Alexandra. (It has now moved to a permanent Alexandra site.) When the door was open to give the class light, it was one with the street. Often people stopped by to say hello and see what was going on. After school we would usually have older state school children come by to paint or draw. Theo tutored high school students and everyone became involved in helping the many families who were dealing with social problems or disasters on the physical plane.

I can't begin to describe the conditions of day-to-day life in the township. The lack of sanitation utilities and safety was a constant drain on families. There was much sickness among the people and the diet staple—corn mush—filled bellies but didn't provide many nutrients. That so many parents came to the school meetings and class nights was a wonder to me. I never left dry-eyed as people appreciated each other and their teachers. An often-expressed concern by American parents has to do with the children being "ready" for high school or college. There they were simply excited by the lights in their children's eyes, by the idea that they could unfold into free-thinking human beings. They had confidence they would learn the academics—it was the way Waldorf looks at child development that really made sense to them.

Claartje and I took a trip to Kwa Zulu. We stayed on the biodynamic farm that is home to a state-funded Waldorf school. Looking out over the hills in the early morning, watching the children walking to school through the fields was an incredible experience. They all stood outside singing for half an hour—this was standard practice at every school we visited—and then separated into various combinations of classes. The rural schools have their own challenges to deal with. Most teachers have only a grade school education. They have had only a basic training themselves and materials are scarce. Children enter school at all ages, so you might have a ten-year-old coming to first grade. Many children live in huts without lights, making it difficult to study at night.

The four teachers carried on as best they could between Baobab visits, but they weren't able to progress very far by themselves, even with constant support by the farmers. We worked with the teachers for three days, helping with lesson preparation, going over the basics of Waldorf education. We also taught non-stop in the classroom. Again, the children were incredibly responsible. Looking at the artwork, I was touched to see how the teachers tried to blend their training with Waldorf themes for the different ages.

This past year two couples from northern Europe arrived at the farm to work in the school. Because of the Zulu violence, one night over 200 children arrived needing a home. As of now there are more than 400 children attending the Meadowsweet School.

Emily, one of the original kindergarten teachers, decided to take Waldorf education back to her village. She went to England for three months to work with Margret Meyerkort and then returned to Maebelo, a village nestled in the mountains of the northern "homelands." We had to receive permission from the chief to visit and we arrived just in time to join a funeral procession of a young man killed in Soweto. We spent several hours singing while the grave was dug. When they were moved to do so, people spoke about the boy. Everyone was huddled together to find relief from the cold. From the cemetery I could see the village. The outsides of many houses were painted in geometric designs, and the wooden fences around animals were put together in a way that made them look like living sculptures.

We visited Emily's kindergarten—30 children at that time. Their circle was in English, Zulu and Sesotho. Their nature garden was filled with African vegetation, and Whitsunday doves hung from above. The community group that serves to support the kindergarten came to meet us. Again, Emily could not be there without community support. None of the support group are parents, just interested neighbors. The chief came with a delegation to meet us, stayed all day, and told wonderful tales of the elementals that live in their mountains. Claartje and I met with the local principal and a few teachers. We gave an impromptu session on creative grammar and math. They asked us to return for a few days of intensive study. Everywhere we went it was an often-repeated request. People were very open and hungry for Waldorf ideas. There were always requests for help from little groups forming here and there.

The Baobab trainers were constantly busy. Between planning meetings and community work, our days were filled, and there was always the feeling that there was so much more to do.

During the summer of 1989, I attended a historic conference, the S.A. national teachers' conference in Cape Town. It was historic because it was the first time Black and White teachers met as colleagues. From my outside vantage point, I found it amazing to observe the changes occurring during the conference. Relations seemed distant until an evening sharing. There many of the Baobab-trained teachers shared what they were doing and the challenges they were up against. It was very moving, and from then on I sensed an acceptance of these new initiatives. The Black teachers brought a richness to the meetings with their singing and speaking that I felt grounded the conference in Africa.

The South African Waldorf community is grappling with its future direction. The established schools which follow a traditional curriculum support the teacher training center. They would like all teachers to receive a complete teacher training. Baobab is trying to answer the immediate needs of the community, providing continuing education and support to people enthusiastically getting on with the work.

I know that since that conference, the established schools here have really reached out into the Black-Colored communities around them. Baobab tries to have as many teachers in the Cape Town training center as their fundraising can support. Things are moving at a quick pace as politics allow new possibilities. I look forward to the day when the rich traditions of Africa are commonplace in all the schools.

Note: Truus Geraets now lives in Southern California and is affiliated with The Waldorf School of Orange County. Her center for the Art of Living is there.

Cultural Diversity and the Universal Human

Joan Almon, Alliance for Childhood

When Betty Staley, editor of this journal, asked me to organize an issue on the Waldorf kindergarten in relation to the multicultural impulse, I had no idea what a challenge lay ahead. Two years later I am beginning to realize that multiculturalism is one of the richest and most complex issues we have undertaken as Waldorf educators.

Five years ago, most Waldorf teachers felt that they were bringing their children a much wider, more diverse picture of the world than was generally found in other schools in America. In most cases this feeling was valid, for generally what one usually found in American schools then was a media-dominated form of pop culture. In contrast, Waldorf students were being introduced to age-old fairy tales, folk tales, myths, poems and songs that have enriched human culture for hundreds and even thousands of years.

Yet on closer inspection, we found, at least in the kindergarten, that while we were bringing archetypal pictures through diverse stories, songs and verse, they were drawn primarily from various parts of Europe and from the European-American culture. Relatively little thought was being given to how the great archetypal pictures manifest in the cultures of Africa, Asia, Latin

America and in Native American life. Now we are in the 1990s, and we ask ourselves, is the old way enough? If not, what else is needed? How can more be brought without awakening the young child prematurely? What is it that the young child needs from us?

We know both from Rudolf Steiner's indications and from contemporary events that this decade will be fraught with social difficulties. Whether the spotlight is on Yugoslavia, Northern Ireland, or Los Angeles, we see one group splitting from another and responding to age-old pain with great violence. We know that through imitation young children absorb a great deal from their environment and from the thoughts and feelings of the adults around them. Are today's kindergarten children to grow up with a sense that the human family is falling apart, is so dysfunctional that it is turning against itself and destroying itself? Is there a counter image that we, as kindergarten teachers and parents, can offer the children of a human family at peace with itself, respecting each of its members, recognizing the unique gifts of each and benefiting from those gifts?

The peoples of the earth are incredibly diverse, and it is wonderful to consider why there is so much diversity in the world. Wouldn't it be much easier if the Creator had made mankind more homogeneous? We have enough difficulty finding our way to one another as two genders. Must we also have so many races, ethnic groups, religions and languages? Yet there is something about the earth and the way life develops here that calls for great diversity. This may seem a poor example, but I remember standing in front of display cases in a tiny museum in Germany which showed dozens, if not hundreds, of different forms of roaches. For the first time I was really struck by how diverse life on the earth is, and this is only one creature among millions which inhabit the earth. If even so lowly a creature is gifted with such diversity, how much more precious must be the diversity of mankind?

In the plant kingdom we see the same impulse to diversify, and if we are sensitive to plants, we can feel the different qualities each brings to the earth. Consider the striking contrast between the white lily and the red rose; the one appears so upright with a quiet dignity while the other is so robust and full of energy. Some souls may identify more with one than with the other, but ultimately both qualities live within each of us and the most well-balanced person is the one who recognizes and cultivates both qualities. Just as our bodies need both the life-filled red blood as well as the cooler, less regenerative forces of the nervous system, so, too, we need the qualities of the red rose and the white lily in our being.

Perhaps this example gives a key to understanding why there is such diversity among human groups. Each of us is complex and unique, and many streams dwell simultaneously within us. We listen not only to our own drummer, but also to the rhythms of many drums. Can we be still and feel the rhythms of Africa and Asia coursing through us, of Europe and of the Americas? Diversity exists not only outside of us, but most profoundly inside of us, as well. To concern ourselves with cultural diversity is to know others more fully, but it is also to know ourselves. Just as learning a foreign language makes us more aware of our own, so knowing another culture makes us more conscious of our own. Such knowledge of self and of others can provide a new basis for social relations, a new basis for peace. Is this hope just a dream for the future, or are there practical inner steps we can take along the way to such knowledge?

Rudolf Steiner, with his deep insights into the spiritual nature of the human being, describes an essential step when he says that there comes a point in human development when we cease to identify so strongly with our own birth group, the group we are connected to through blood ties. We become, spiritually speaking, homeless and feel ourselves more at home in the wide world than in our own land or culture. Many of us can identify with this feeling, for it is our experience as modern human beings to move more freely over the earth and find our rightful spiritual home rather than being limited to the space in which we were born. Indeed, it is because this impulse of spiritual rootlessness is so strong that we sometimes shy away from many of the manifestations of multiculturalism in our society. Some of it seems like a hearkening back to an older time when human consciousness was largely shaped by the thoughts and feelings of one's blood group, be it family, race or nationality. We recognize that today we must be present as individuals, each developing our own consciousness, though within a healthy social life.

Homelessness, however, is only one step along the way for the evolving soul. Rudolf Steiner says that at the next stage we need to come to know our own group, our folk-soul, in a new way. We now approach our roots with consciousness. In the first lecture of *The Mission of Folk-Souls* (1910), Steiner reminds us that in ancient Greece above the Apollonian Mystery Centers there stood the words, "Man Know Thyself." In the not far distant future, Steiner said in this lecture, the folk-souls themselves will be challenged to *know* themselves. "Folk Soul Know Thyself" will help characterize this new phase and "this saying will have a certain significance for the future work of mankind."

To many of us it seems that the time is now at hand when a greater awareness of our own folk-soul is needed. True, there is always the danger that delving into this realm of consciousness will take us back to a time when we identified only with our own nation or tribe; but without becoming conscious of folk-soul, it will be difficult if not impossible to go forward. My own experience is that turning towards our folk-souls with a new consciousness actually frees us from their ancient bonds. For years I had yearned for a connection to the past of my parents, German Jews who grew up in the Black Forest of southern Germany. When I at last visited these places and met people who recognized my connection to the towns and to my family, I felt freed from the past. I suspect that Alex Haley, who wrote *Roots*, had a similar experience when at last he heard the griot in Africa connect his life with that of his ancestors in the village.

Where does this new freedom lead us? It takes us closer to our own unique individuality and at the same time is a step towards recognizing the universal human being who dwells in all of us. In identifying with the universal, we are able to overcome a great danger which Rudolf Steiner describes in the fourth lecture of *The Universal Human,* a lecture well worth reading for those concerned with questions of race. Here he says that through the negative intervention of Ahriman and Lucifer, beings who continually work to undermine the human being's spiritual development, mankind ran the risk of becoming hardened into racial groups that could no longer reach out to one another. Each race would have become so insular that mankind would have become like the animal species which can co-exist upon the earth simultaneously but with no real understanding of one another. Had we gone in this direction, we would have lost all sense of the universal which unites us as human beings. We would have lost all capacity to love anyone the least bit different from ourselves.

What prevented this great social darkness from occurring was the incarnation of the Logos or the Christ, a being whose task it was to bring love to the earth. If this new capacity for love had not entered the stream of humanity, we would have become totally divided from one another. Now the possibility exists for us to know one another at a much deeper and more profound level. But whether we move in such a direction is up to us, for the capacity to love is closely linked with human freedom. We are free to insulate ourselves into our own groups or to reach beyond—in a new spirit—to one another.

As we watch the events unfold in Bosnia, we see that it is a matter of great significance which direction we choose, backwards towards our blood ties or forwards towards a new, more universal sense of the human being. The old ways do not work for us any longer, not even the old forms of peace which were primarily based on the dominance of one group over another. The times call for new social relationships which have to have a whole new basis. As we live into this decade with its strong potential for social disintegration, we seek a new source of strength so that we can bring about social integration instead. Where do we find this help?

This decade is often described as being apocalyptic, a time full of spiritual awakening but also of earthly chaos. In the following passage Rudolf Steiner points to the great possibilities of these times, for as we stand closer to the threshold of the spirit, we see not only the pitfalls before us but also the path of human growth and evolution, of human healing and transformation. It takes courage to walk this new path which opens before our feet, and it takes an open mind and an open heart to go beyond the old boundaries of race, nationality or religion to experience that which is now coming to birth.

> We have to face calmly and courageously the increasing diversity in human nature because we know that we can carry a word into all these diversities that is not merely a word of speech but one of power. Though there may be groups that fight against each other and though we may even belong to one of them, we know that we can bring something that will express: "It is no longer I who live, but Christ who lives in me" into every group. We know that this "Christ who lives in me" will not lead to the forming of groups; rather, it will bring about the spreading of the glory of the name "human being" over the whole earth.

> The understanding of spiritual science brings to life the realization that we can carry the power that comes from the words, "It is no longer I who live, but Christ

who lives in me" into the groups that are fighting each other—no matter into which group we bring our I.

This is one of the practical and moral-ethical aspects of our strivings in spiritual science. (*The Universal Human*, p. 91)

Chorus for the Coming Age

Arvia MacKaye Ege

New archangelic might
Is pouring from the heavens;
New Christ sight
Is awakening on the earth;
New human light
Is streaming
Through the gates of death and birth.

Out of cataclysmic strife,
The new mysteries of life—
The new light age
Of the Risen One
Has at last begun—

Its myriad redeeming deeds
Flocking to be done;
Its apocalyptic victories—
Wide-winged—waiting to be won!…

Through every dark, its mercy-call
Summons now the hearts of all;
Its living-fingered light unbinds

The frozen shrouds that blind men's minds,
Sets free each will—that everyone
May join the warriors of the sun,
In rescue of that spirit core
That all the universe is for.

From Secret Iron of the Heart, *poems by Arvia MacKaye Ege.*
Reprinted with permission of Adonis Press.

Fairy Tales from around the World

One of the beauties of fairy tales is that the universal world of archetypes speaks through them. One sees remarkably similar pictures in fairy tales from all parts of the world. They speak a universal language, and for the human soul it is a language reminiscent of that spoken before the Tower of Babel twisted our tongues and made our speech incomprehensible to one another. Fairy tales contain a language still understood by human beings all over the earth, both children and adults.

Though universal in nature, fairy tales also carry something of the unique quality of the culture from which they are drawn. Waldorf kindergarten teachers have been seeking tales from diverse cultures to bring to their children, but it is often hard to find tales which are simple enough for the kindergarten. When assessing the appropriateness of a fairy tale for the kindergarten, one consideration is the strength of evil in the tale.

Most fairy tales portray a confrontation between good and evil, but sometimes the force of evil is very strong and is better suited for the older child. One also considers how difficult the tasks of the central figure are in the story. In kindergarten tales, the hero or heroine may have three tasks to do, but if there are more than three, the story is probably better suited to the elementary-aged child. In addition, young children need a sense that goodness prevails and that good triumphs over evil. After telling fairy tales to children for a time, one forgets these criteria and develops a sense for what is appropriate for the children.

We include here several fairy tales which are now being used by Waldorf kindergarten teachers. Initial indications are that minority children, in particular, light up when they hear a story or fairy tale which is drawn from their own culture. They need this quiet acknowledgment of their cultural background and blossom with it. When telling a fairy tale from a culture which is not your own, it is important to have formed a positive relationship to the culture and to the story. Then it will not seem foreign to you or to the children who are hearing it. Through the power of imitation, the children are then able to live into the tale, even when there is no one from that culture in the kindergarten. The Kindergarten Association would like to hear from teachers about their experiences in bringing these tales to the children, both positive experiences as well as difficulties, so that we can learn from one another.

We would also like to continue collecting non-European fairy tales which are appropriate for young children. If you find some, please send them to the Kindergarten Association for possible inclusion in future *Newsletters*. As copyright permission is needed for many of these tales, please send a copy of the front and back of the title page of the book when you send the story.

Akimba and the Magic Cow
A Folktale from Africa

Retold by Ann Rose

In this journal we seek permission to print copyrighted material, but it is not always possible to learn if there is a copyright holder. After corresponding with several publishers, we have been unable to determine who holds the legal copyright for this story. If anyone can clear this matter up for us we would be most grateful. It appears in a picture book entitled Akimba and the Magic Cow, *now out of print, published by Four Seasons Press of New York, a subsidiary of Macmillan Publishers.*

Elaine Harris and Irene Morgan of the Urban Waldorf School in Milwaukee brought this story to our attention when they presented it as a table puppet play at a multicultural conference. The opening paragraph has been added to the original story.

Listen, listen and you will hear the sounds and rhythms of the village and the forest, sounds of nature. The people here still live close to nature. Come experience with me the magic of the sounds and see what happens.

Long ago in a little African village lived a man named Akimba. Akimba was the poorest man in his village. One morning he had nothing left to eat, not even a crumb. *I have no food and I have no money. I must leave the village,* Akimba thought, *and see what I can do.*

So Akimba set out. Soon he came to a deep forest. He saw an old man chopping firewood. Akimba helped him stack the logs. "Where are you going?" the old man asked.

"I have no food and I have no money. I must see what I can do," Akimba said.

"Maybe I can help you," said the old man. "Behind this bush you'll find a cow. Take her home with you and say 'kukuku.' Say 'kukuku' to her and see what happens."

So Akimba took the cow and went back to his hut. "Kukuku," he said to her. The cow opened her mouth and a gold coin fell out. "Wah!" cried Akimba. "Kukuku! Kukuku!" And in no time at all, Akimba was rich.

One day Akimba had to go on a long journey. He could not take his cow with him. So he went to see his good neighbor Bumba. "Bumba," he said, "will you keep my cow for me? She's no trouble as long as you don't say 'kukuku' to her. 'Kukuku' is the one thing you must never say."

"Very well," Bumba said. "I will do as you wish."

So Akimba gave Bumba the cow and went down the road. The very moment Akimba was gone, Bumba ran up to the cow. "Kukuku," he said. To his amazement the cow opened her mouth and a gold coin fell out. "Kukuku," Bumba said again. Another coin fell to the ground. "Wah!" cried Bumba. "This cow is good to have and better to keep."

A few days later, Akimba came back. "Where is my cow?" he asked.

"Here she is," Bumba said. But he gave Akimba another cow instead.

Akimba took the cow home and said, "Kukuku."

"Moo-oo," said the cow, but nothing happened. "Have you forgotten your master's voice?" Akimba shouted. "Kuku, kukuku!"

"Moo-oo, moooo-oooo," mooed the cow. But no gold coins came.

So Akimba went to find the old man in the woods. "My cow stopped giving gold," Akimba said. "Soon I will be hungry again."

"Behind this bush you'll find a sheep. Take her home with you and say 'bururu.' Say 'bururu' to her and see what happens."

So Akimba took the sheep and went back to his hut. "Bururu," he said to her. The sheep opened her mouth and a silver coin fell out. "Wah!" Akimba shouted. "Bururu, bururu!" And in no time at all, Akimba was rich.

But the day came when Akimba had to leave on another journey. He brought his sheep to his good neighbor Bumba. "Bumba," he asked, "will you keep my sheep for me? She's no trouble as long as you don't say 'bururu' to her. 'Bururu' is the one thing you must never say."

"Very well," Bumba said. "I will do as you wish."

The moment Akimba was gone, Bumba ran to the sheep. "Bururu!" he said. The sheep opened her mouth. A silver coin fell out. "Wah!" Bumba shouted. "This sheep is good to have and better yet to keep."

A few weeks later, Akimba came back. "Where is my sheep?" he asked.

"Here she is," said Bumba. But he gave Akimba another sheep instead.

Akimba hurried home. "Bururu," he said to the sheep.

"Baa, baa," said the sheep. But no silver coins fell.

"Bururu! Bururu!" Akimba shouted. Still no silver coins! "This sheep has turned deaf in my absence," said Akimba. And he went to find the old man in the woods.

"My sheep stopped giving silver," Akimba said. "Soon I'll be as hungry as before."

"There is a chicken behind this bush. Take her with you," said the old man. "When you get home, say 'klaklakla' to her, say 'klaklakla' and see what happens."

So Akimba got the chicken and took her home. "Klaklakla," he said to her. The chicken laid an egg. "What?" yelled Akimba. "No silver? No gold? Klaklakla," he shouted. The chicken laid more eggs. "Well," said Akimba, "eggs are eggs." And he ate them.

The next time he was called away, he asked Bumba to keep his chicken. "She's no trouble as long as you don't say 'klaklakla' to her. 'Klaklakla' is the one thing you must never say."

"Do not worry," Bumba said. "I will be more than glad to keep your chicken."

As soon as Akimba was out of sight, Bumba ran to the chicken. "Klaklakla!" he shouted. The chicken laid an egg. "Fooh!" cried Bumba. "No gold? No silver? Only eggs?" *Oh well,* he thought, *eggs are eggs.* And he ate them.

And when Akimba came back and asked for his chicken, Bumba gave him another one instead.

So Akimba went to see the old man in the woods again. "My cow stopped giving gold," he cried. "My sheep stopped giving silver. Even my chicken stopped laying eggs. Soon I will be as hungry as before."

"There's a stick behind the bush," the old man said. "Go home and tell it to dance for you. When you want it to stop say 'mulu.'"

"Thank you," said Akimba, and he took the stick.

As soon as he was home, he told the stick to dance. But the stick did not dance. It jumped up and beat him instead. Akimba was so surprised he almost forgot the magic word. "Mulu!" he yelled at last, and the stick fell to the floor. Akimba looked at the stick for a long time. *Hmmm,* he thought. *I must pay another visit to Bumba.* Then Akimba took the stick to Bumba's house.

"Bumba," he said, "I have to leave again. Will you keep the stick for me?"

"Well, well," Bumba thought. "The cow brought me gold. The sheep brought me silver. The chicken brought me eggs. Who knows what the stick will bring?" And he grabbed the stick and pushed Akimba out the door.

Akimba turned around. "I almost forgot," he said. "Do not say 'Stick, dance for me.' Remember, whatever you do, do not ask the stick to dance."

The moment Akimba was out of sight Bumba yelled, "Stick, dance for me!" And the stick jumped up. But it did not dance. It beat him and beat him and would not stop. The stick was still beating Bumba when Akimba came back.

"Now will you give me my true cow and my true sheep and my true chicken?" Akimba asked.

"Anything!" cried Bumba. "Just stop this stick from beating me!"

"Mulu," Akimba said. And the stick fell to the floor.

Akimba picked up the stick. He took his true cow and his true sheep. He took his true chicken. Then he went back to his hut. "Klaklakla," he said to his chicken. Akimba's plate was filled with eggs. "Bururu," he said to his sheep. And silver coins clanked to the floor. "Kukuku," he said to his cow. And gold coins piled up to the roof.

Akimba never had to go hungry again.

The Winning of Kwelanga
A Zulu Tale

Near the Mountains of the Dragon, there once lived a great chief named Ngazulu. He had a daughter who was so beautiful and gentle that she was called Kwelanga, which means sunrise. It was the chief's desire that Kwelanga be married to a man worthy of her. So all suitors were put to impossible tests. Naturally all failed to win her.

One day a young man named Zamo heard about this. At once he decided to try his luck. His father tried to dissuade him. He said, "We are poor people. How dare you think of marrying the daughter of the chief?"

His mother said, "Oh, Zamo! Every man who has tried has lost his life. Do you think you would fare any better?"

But Zamo said, "I can't whistle with another's mouth. I must try it myself."

So one day Zamo went to Chief Ngazulu and said, "Greetings, Nkosi." Then he waited for the chief to speak.

The chief said, "Young man, what are you doing here? Have you lost your way?"

"No, Nkosi," said Zamo, "this is the end of my journey. I have come to propose marriage with your daughter."

"You come, with no attendants, to propose marriage?" cried the chief.

"Nkosi," said Zamo humbly, "it is the custom of my people to act alone."

"Proposer-of-marriage," said the chief, "are you prepared to do the tasks we will set for you?"

"I am here to try," said Zamo.

Ngazulu said, "Well then, look yonder. Do you see that cultivated field? Kaffir corn has been sown there. Before sundown you must gather all the grain that has been scattered. Then you may speak to me of marriage."

At that moment Kwelanga passed by on her way to the stream to draw water. She swayed gracefully beneath the earthen pot balanced on her head. When she saw the handsome suitor talking with her father, she began humming a little tune.

When the young man saw Kwelanga, he thought she was as pretty as a sunbird. He said, "Let me begin at once."

Zamo went straight to the field. Finding a huge basket nearby, he took it and began picking up the kernels of kaffir corn. He worked all day without resting. When the sun was about to disappear in the west, he still hadn't finished half the field.

Just then he heard someone singing from the hillside above him:

> "Red grains of Kaffir corn
> Scattered by our mothers,
> Fly back from whence you came,
> Gather with the others."

Suddenly the basket was heaped with grain. Zamo looked about and saw that the field was clean. He knew that every kernel had returned to the basket, and he carried the grain to Ngazulu.

When the chief saw the filled basket, he said, "You did well, young man. But that task was too easy. Tomorrow we shall talk again."

Zamo was given food and a hut in which to sleep. Very early the following morning he went to sit near the chief's door. When Ngazulu came out, he said, "Young man, what do you want with me?"

Zamo said, "Nkosi, I have come to propose marriage at this kraal."

The chief said, "See that forest in the valley? If you are able to chop down all the trees before sunset, then come to me and talk of marriage."

Zamo fetched an axe and went to the forest. He set to work with all speed. Many trees fell before his axe. But the forest was large, and though he worked all day without rest, most of the trees were still left. As the sun was slipping behind the hill, he heard a sweet voice singing:

"Trees of the forest,
In the sun's red glow,
Fall before Zamo—
Bow yourselves low."

At that, the trees crashed down on every side. Not one was left standing. Just then the sun set. Zamo went to the chief and said, "Nkosi, have I not finished the task you gave me?"

The chief was very much surprised. He called his counselor and said, "Think of something really hard for this man to do. The tasks I have given him have been too easy."

The counselor put his hand over his mouth, as is the way with people deep in thought. Then he said, "Let Zamo come to us in the morning. We will think of something that is not so easy."

The chief and his counselor sat up all night discussing what trial to give the young man. Just as the sun was rising they came to a decision. When Zamo appeared, the counselor said, "Young man, do you see that thorn tree growing out from the edge of the cliff, the one way up high on the mountainside? You are to climb out on it and pluck the topmost thorn."

Zamo saw the scraggly tree growing out from a crag high up on the mountain. *No one could climb out on that*, he thought. But he said nothing and set off up a steep mountain path.

The chief and his counselor watched him go. They were sure that Zamo would not be able to climb the tree because of the thorns. Even if he should manage to crawl out on it, the tree would bend with his weight and surely throw him off into the gorge. In any event, they thought they had seen the last of him.

When Zamo reached the edge of the cliff, he looked down to see what lay beneath the thorn tree. Far, far down he saw nothing but gray rubble—the rocks of all sizes that had rolled down the mountain. He knew that to fall would mean certain death.

The trunk of the thorn tree angled outward and upward from the cliff. Zamo began to creep out on it, picking his way between big thorns. As he neared the twisted umbrella of branches, the thorns were so close together that there was no place even for fingertips. Then the tree began to bend. Zamo stopped breathing, and with great difficulty made his way back to the foot of the tree. Just then he heard a voice singing behind him:

> "Thorn tree, thorn tree,
> Wind and weather worn tree,
> Your topmost thorn, please
> Pluck for Zamo and me."

Suddenly a small gray thorn came twirling through the air. It landed beside Zamo. He picked it up and, turning quickly, he saw Kwelanga coming toward him with outstretched hands. He knew at once that it was she who had sung the magic songs that had helped him every time.

Zamo took Kwelanga's hand, and together they went to her father.

"Nkosi," said Zamo, "here is the topmost thorn. I have finished the tasks. Kwelanga is willing, and I have come to propose marriage at this kraal."

When Ngazulu saw the look of happiness on the face of his daughter, he knew that Zamo truly was worthy of her. For he knew that the best husband for a woman is the man who can make her happy.

The Winning of Kwelanga

The Silent Maiden
A Tale from East Africa

Told by Eleanor B. Heady

This tale was sent to us by Ann Pratt of the Waldorf Urban Program in Milwaukee. It is from the book When the Stones Were Soft *by Eleanor B. Heady. This book is no longer in print, and we have been unable to locate the holder of its copyright. If anyone can provide information about this, we would be most grateful. In the introduction to this story, Eleanor Heady says that the tale goes back at least to the sixth century AD, for it is found in* The Panchatantra. *It is similar to the "Golden Goose" in the Grimms' collection, but here the maiden must speak not laugh, and this is accomplished through a trick.*

Once very long ago, there was a beautiful young maiden called Mepo. She was the daughter of the great chief, Amagogo. Mepo was good and handsome, with skin like black velvet, teeth like flashing pearls, eyes with a dark diamond brightness. Her smile made all who saw her love her. Because of her great beauty, she was her father's favorite daughter.

When it came time for Mepo to marry, she went to her father and said, "Father, please do not give me to the first man who offers you a great reward, nor to any man you fancy, but let me choose my own husband. He must be handsome, a valiant warrior, a fine hunter, and clever."

"A man like that would make a very good husband indeed. If you are looking for such a man, you may certainly choose for yourself," said the chief.

So word went out to the other villages that the young men of the tribe might pay court to Mepo, the beautiful daughter of the chief, Amagogo. They came from miles around, short men, tall men, lean men, fat men, young men, and old men. All of them tried so hard to please the girl that she became very tired of their constant attentions. At last she refused to speak to any of them.

"Daughter, why do you behave so?" asked her father. "Your mother and I are worried because you do not speak." Mepo shook her head wearily and refused to say a word.

Still the young men and the old men came. For weeks the spears stuck into the ground at the door of the chief's house told all who passed by that there were many men visiting Mepo. But she only sat in the center of the admiring circle and smiled sadly. They brought her gifts of ripe fruit, melons, choice meat, and beads of many colors. But still she refused to speak to anyone or to choose between them.

Finally her father tired of this stubborn behavior. He sent out word to the villages that he would give Mepo in marriage to anyone who could make her speak.

In a village faraway across the great river lived a brave young chief of another tribe. His name was Fupajena. He heard of the silent maiden and of her father's offer. He went to the village and asked at the house of Amagogo for permission to meet her. The old chief welcomed him. Such a strong and handsome young man would make a fine husband for his daughter.

"How I hope you can make her speak," said Amagogo. "I'm sure she would be happy with you."

Fupajena was shown into the chief's hut. Mepo looked up wearily from her basket making. "Great beauty is yours, lovely Mepo," said Fupajena with a low bow. "Will you be my wife?"

Mepo lowered her eyes and refused to say a word.

Fupajena had come a long way to pay court to the beautiful maiden. Amagogo had a bed of skins made for him inside one of the houses and invited him to spend the night.

It was weeding time, for the rains had just passed. Early the next morning Mepo took her hoe and went to weed her maize field.

Fupajena watched her go, then quietly followed. When they reached the field, Fupajena again said to her, "Please, beautiful Mepo, be my wife."

Mepo did not answer, but handed him the hoe and went and sat in the shade of a tree. The young chief began hoeing with quick sure strokes. "Look, Mepo" he called. "I have finished."

Mepo looked at the field. She shouted angrily, "Punda, donkey! You have ruined my crop. You hoed up the maize and left the weeds standing!"

Fupajena threw down the hoe and began to dance and laugh. Mepo became angrier and shouted louder than before. "How could anyone be so stupid?"

In mock fright, the young chief ran toward Amagogo's house. Mepo followed, still shouting. Her father and mother hearing the noise, met them outside. They were overjoyed that someone had made their daughter speak.

After her anger cooled, Mepo knew that Fupajena had been clever enough to make her forget her silence. She gladly went home with him to be his wife and was never silent again.

The Moon Maiden
A Japanese Fairy Tale

From My Book House, *which is no longer in print. If anyone has copyright information on this story, please let us know. Nancy Foster of Acorn Hill gave us this story and points out that it is reminiscent of "The Snow Maiden." The two stories are good examples of how a similar fairy tale motif can be clothed in a delicate Oriental garment or a wintry Russian one. This is a particularly lovely story for the late spring or early summer when the fireflies have begun to glow.*

There dwelt once on the edge of the forest at the foot of Fujiyama, a bamboo-cutter and his wife. They were honest, industrious people who loved each other dearly, but no children had come to bless them, and therefore they were not happy.

"Ah, husband," mourned the wife, "more welcome to me than cherry blossoms in springtime would be a little child of my own."

One evening she stood on the porch of her flimsy bamboo cottage and lifted her eyes toward the everlasting snows on the top of Fujiyama. Then, with swelling breast, she bowed herself to the ground and cried out to the Honorable Mountain: "Fuji no yama, I am sad because no little head lies on my breast, no childish laughter gladdens our home. Send me, I pray thee, from thine eternal purity, a little one to comfort me."

As she spoke, lo! from the top of the Honorable Mountain there suddenly sparked a gleam of light as when the face of a child is lit by a beaming smile. "Husband, husband, come quickly," cried the good woman. "See there on the heights of Fujiyama a child is beaming upon me."

"It is but your fancy," said the bamboo-cutter, and yet he added, "I will climb up and see what is there." So he followed the trail of silvery light through the forest and up the steep slope where Fujiyama towered white and still above him. At last he stopped below a tall bamboo by the bank of a mountain stream from whence the glow seemed to come. There, cradled in the branches of the tree, he found a tiny moon-child, fragile, dainty, radiant, clad in flimsy, filmy moonshine, more beautiful than anything he had ever seen before.

"Ah, little shining creature, who are you?" he cried.

"I am the Princess Moonbeam," answered the child. "The Moon Lady is my mother, but she has sent me to earth to comfort the sad heart of your wife."

"Then, little Princess," said the man eagerly, "I will take you home to be our child." So the woodman bore her carefully down the mountain side.

"See, wife," he called, "what the Moon Lady has sent you." Then was the good woman overjoyed. She took the little moon-child and held her close, and the moon-child's little arms went twining about her neck, as she nestled snug against her breast. So was the good wife's longing satisfied at last.

As the years passed by, Princess Moonbeam brought nothing but joy to the woodman and his wife. Lovelier and lovelier she grew. Fair was her face and radiant, her eyes were shining stars, and her hair had the gleam of a misty silver halo. About her, too, there was a strange, unearthly charm that made all who saw her love her.

One day there came riding by in state the Mikado himself. He saw how the Princess Moonbeam lit up the humble cottage, and he loved her. Then the Mikado would have taken her back with him to court, but no!—the longing of the earthly father and mother for a little child had been fulfilled, the Princess Moonbeam had stayed with them till she was a maiden grown, and now the time had come when she must go back to her sky mother, the Lady in the Moon.

"Stay, stay with me on earth!" cried the Mikado.

"Stay, stay with us on earth!" cried the bamboo-cutter and his wife.

Then the Mikado got two thousand archers and set them on guard close about the house and even on the roof, that none might get through to take her. But when the moon rose white and full, a line of light like a silver bridge sprung arching down from heaven to earth and floating along that gleaming path came the Lady from the Moon. The Mikado's soldiers stood as though turned to stone. Straight through their midst the Moon Lady passed and bent caressingly down for her long-absent child. She wrapped her close in a garment of silver mist. Then she caught her tenderly in her arms and led her gently back to the sky.

The Princess Moonbeam was glad to go back home, yet as she went, she wept silvery tears for those she was leaving behind. And lo! her bright, shining tears took wings and floated away to carry a message of love, that should comfort the Mikado and her earthly father and mother.

To this very day the gleaming tears of the little Princess Moonbeam are seen to float hither and yon about the marshes and groves of Japan. The children chase them with happy cries and say, "See the fireflies! How beautiful they are!" Then their mothers, in the shadow of Fujiyama, tell the children this legend—how the fireflies are shining love messages of the little Princess Moonbeam, flitting down to bring comfort to earth from her home in the silver moon.

The Arrow Chain
A Tlingit Tale

This story was adapted by Susan Howard of the Waldorf Institute of Sunbridge College for use in the kindergarten as a marionette play with music.

There were once two boys, a chief's son and his best friend, who lived together in the same village and always played together. They spent their days making arrows out of feathers and birch twigs, and walking in the countryside around their village. One summer night, they set out for their playing fields and walked across a large, grassy field. The moon was full and very bright, and almost seemed to be watching them.

"Look at the moon," said the friend, laughing. "How silly and ugly it looks with all those marks all over its face!"

"Hush," whispered the chief's son. "You mustn't say things like that about the moon!"

As soon as he had spoken, a huge shadow swept over the field, and a strange, shimmering rainbow appeared out of the shadow and settled around his friend. When it disappeared, his friend was gone.

He called and called to him, but there was no answer. *The moon has taken him*, he thought, and sat down on the hillside and cried. When he had no more tears, he looked up at the sky and saw a large, bright star beside the moon. *I am going to aim for that star*, he thought. He took out his bow and arrow and, aiming very carefully, he shot at the star. In a moment the star disappeared, and the arrow did not return. Encouraged, he pulled out another arrow, and over and over again, he shot in the same direction, at the place where the star had been. He used nearly all of the arrows that he and his friend had made.

When almost all the arrows were gone, he looked and saw something hanging from the sky, very close to him. It was a chain of arrows, one fastened to the other. He shot a few more, until the chain almost reached the ground, and just as he shot the last arrow, the sun began to rise. As its first rays touched the chain of arrows, it became a ladder, leading up to the sky.

The chief's son decided to climb up. First, he took some berry bush branches and stuck them into his hair. He climbed and climbed all day and camped on the ladder at nightfall. In the morning when he awoke his head felt heavy. He pulled out the branches and they were filled with ripe berries. He ate and ate, felt strengthened and continued climbing.

By the time he reached the top, he was very tired. He looked around and saw a large lake and lay down beside it and fell asleep. In his sleep he heard a small voice speaking to him, saying, "Wake up, I am coming for you." He opened his eyes and saw a little girl standing beside him.

"I have come to take you to my grandmother," said the girl. "She has been watching you climb up from the earth." And so the chief's son followed the little girl through the sky country until they came to the grandmother's house.

The old woman welcomed them. "You are brave to come up here to the sky country," she said. "What do you seek here?"

"I have come to find my friend," said the chief's son.

"Yes, I know," said the old woman. "He has been captured by the moon, whose house is very near here. We can hear him crying."

They listened and heard his voice, calling out. "I must go to him!" cried the chief's son.

"Wait," said the old woman. "First you must have food, for you are weak from hunger." She raised her hand to her mouth, and a roasted fish appeared upon it. She raised it again, and there was a toasted ear of corn. A third time she raised it, and it was laden with fresh fruit. The chief's son ate hungrily, and soon felt strong and refreshed.

"Now," said the grandmother, "when you go to the house of the Moon, you must take four things." She handed him a pine cone, a fish eye, a rose, and a small piece of stone. Then she and the girl wished him good luck and stood at the door of their house as he hurried away into the land of the moon.

He could hear his friend crying from high up and saw his head sticking out of the smoke hole. He climbed up onto the roof, stepping softly so that the moon could not hear him. His friend was so glad to see him that he stopped crying. "Don't stop!" the chief's son whispered. "The moon mustn't know I am taking you away!" So his friend cried on as he pulled him out of the smoke hole. He pushed the pine cone into his place, and it began to wail just as his friend had done. Then, hand in hand, they jumped down from the roof and started to run.

But soon the pine cone fell into the fire and stopped wailing. The moon realized he had been tricked and set off after them, much faster than they could run. (Music) The chief's son tossed the fish eye behind him, and where it fell a large lake appeared. The moon fell into the water and had to crawl out and roll all the way around the lake after them. (Music)

The chief's son then tossed the rose behind him. A rosebush appeared and caught the moon in its thorns. Slowly the moon struggled free and soon he was close behind them again. (Music)

The chief's son tossed the little stone behind him and a giant mountain appeared. It was so steep that the moon could not climb it, but kept rolling back down, again and again.

At last the two friends reached the grandmother's house. They were very glad to be together again. They thanked her for all the help she had given them and said they longed to be back on the earth again. The grandmother said, "You may return to the earth whenever you wish."

Bidding the old woman goodbye, the two friends walked across the sky country until they came to the top of the ladder. There they lay down, longing to be back home again, and fell asleep. When they awoke, they found themselves back home again on the hillside. They were greeted with cries of joy by their friends and families from the village. They led long and happy lives. And people came from all around to hear their wonderful story.

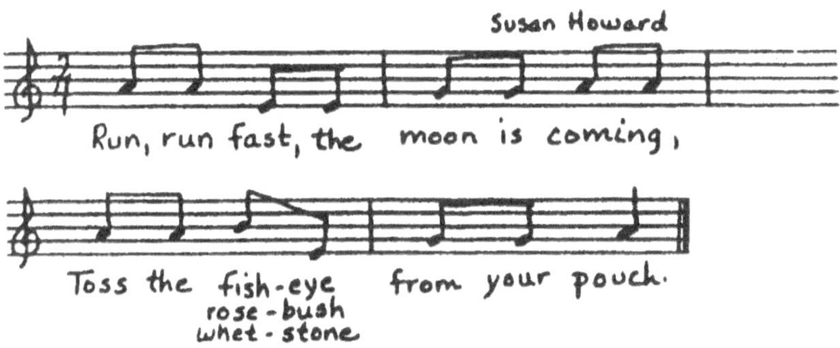

The Invisible Hunter
A Micmac Indian Legend

This story is also known as "The Little Scarred One" or "Burnt One" and is a variation on the Cinderella theme. It was sent to us by several different people including Anna Rainville from California, Ann Pratt from Milwaukee, and Kristi Busch from Seattle. Susan Howard adapted the story with her kindergarten trainees at the Waldorf Institute for use as a marionette play and found songs for it in a book called American Indian Tales and Songs *by Dorothy Gordon, E.P. Dutton & Co., 1933. As there was not time to seek copyright permission for these songs, they are not included in this volume.*

At the far end of a tiny Indian village, where the rosy light of the rising sun played on the ripples of Neganish Bay, lived an old Indian of the Wabanaki with his three daughters. It was the duty of the two elder girls to keep the wigwam in order, cooking the food and dressing the skins for the family's clothing; but they were lazy and shiftless and left most of the work to the youngest girl. Her father called her Little Wonban which means Little Rising Sun, but she was not joyful like the rising sun. She was thin and sad-eyed and wore shabby clothes. Her elder sisters kicked and pushed her about and made her do most of the work, until she often fell asleep from sheer weariness. Sometimes she would fall asleep over the fire, and her face was scarred from the hot cinders. Her long black hair looked dull from the ashes, not shining and sleek like that of her sisters. Since there never seemed to be enough skins when her father came back from the hunt to clothe all of the family, Little Rising Sun had only scraps to wrap about her.

One evening by the fire, the old father told his daughters the story of a mighty warrior and hunter named Te-Am (Great Moose) who lived at the far end of the village. His sister kept his lodge for him, since she was his only living relative. One day, as Te-Am was walking in the forest, a great Chinu came to protect him and to give him a special gift. With this gift, Te-Am had the power to take on the form of a moose. And with this gift he could also make himself invisible. So it was that none of the maidens in the village had ever seen him, though he was said to be very handsome, and his lodge was always well provided with food and soft furs.

Now the father continued his story. "Te-Am's sister has announced that Te-Am wishes to be married. He will take as his wife the first maiden who can see him. Many maidens have already come to his lodge, but none have been able to see him. Now you, my daughters, may go and try your luck."

As the elder sisters heard their father's story, they became very excited and each wanted to go to the lodge of Te-Am. The next morning the eldest sister dressed herself in her best robes with strings of shells around her throat and walked through the village to the lodge of Te-Am. Te-Am's sister received her kindly and entertained her in the lodge until sunset. Then, when it was time for Te-Am to return from the hunt, his sister invited the girl to walk with her down the road that led from the forest.

As soon as she saw her brother approaching, for to her he was always visible, she asked the girl, "Do you see my brother coming?"

Although she could not see him, the girl pretended to and said, "Yes, I can see him."

"Tell me," asked Te-Am's sister, "of what is his great bow made?"

"Of birch wood," answered the girl, although she could not see it. By the girl's answer the sister knew she had not seen her brother, but she said to her, "Since you see him, let us go back to the wigwam."

(Music: humming melody from "Do you see…")

Back in the wigwam, she invited the girl to be seated on her side of the great fire. Then her brother entered and went to his side of the lodge. As he dropped his catch of game to the ground, the girl could see it. And when he drew off his wet moccasins and handed them to his sister, the girl could see them as soon as they touched the sister's hand. But Te-Am she could not see. Sadly, she gave up and went home.

The next day the second sister wanted to try her luck. She too dressed in her finest robes with strings of shells around her neck and walked through the village to the great lodge of Te-Am. She, too, was greeted kindly by his sister. At sunset, she, too, walked with her down the road to see the great hunter return from the forest with his catch of game.

(Music: "Do you see…")

Like her sister, she, too, could not see Te-Am, although she also pretended to. When Te-Am's sister asked her, "Do you see my brother coming along the path?" she answered, "Yes, I see him."

"Of what is his great bow made?" asked the sister of Te-Am.

"Of ash wood," replied the second sister, although she could not see it.

"Since you see my brother, let us go back to the wigwam," said Te-Am's sister.

(Music: humming the melody, "Do you see…")

When Te-Am stepped into the wigwam, the girl could not see him, but again, when his catch of game fell from his shoulder to the ground, she could see it. And when his sister handed him some food to eat, as soon as he touched it, the girl could no longer see it. Finally, she, too, returned to her own wigwam, disappointed.

The two elder sisters talked continuously of the lodge of Te-Am and his sister, until Little Rising Sun decided that she, too, must have a glimpse of that wonderful wigwam. The eldest sister laughed, saying, "How can such a mouse as you hope to see Te-Am, when even we could catch no glimpse of him?"

"Nay," answered Little Rising Sun, "while it may be that I cannot see the mighty hunter, I hope that his sister will receive me and I may catch a glimpse of the beautiful lodge with its rich robes of fur, of which all the maidens speak."

The sisters said no more, but they would not lend Little Rising Sun a dress, and she had to make one of birch bark. Upon her feet she wore her father's old moccasins. Nevertheless, she started out, and did not listen to her sisters' unkind words as they made fun of her strange dress and the misfit moccasins.

Of course I shall not be able to see Te-Am, she thought, *but just to help prepare his supper and see that wonderful wigwam will be joy enough to remember for many days.*

At last she came to the wigwam. While she hesitated at the entrance, the sister of Te-Am saw her and welcomed her in kindly fashion, asking her to sit by the fire. Soon she had her talking about her life at home, but Little Rising Sun said nothing of the unkindness of her sisters to her. At sunset, the two maidens walked towards the forest.

(Music: "Do you see…")

When the sister saw her brother coming, she said, "Te-Am is coming. Can you see him yonder on the path?"

Looking toward the forest Little Rising Sun opened her eyes in wonder as she replied, "Yes, I see the shining one."

"Tell me then," replied the sister, "of what is his hunter's bow made that he carries in his hand?"

"It is the rainbow!" whispered Little Rising Sun.

"Ah, then you do truly see my brother," replied his sister. "Now let us hasten home and prepare for his coming."

So the two maidens hurried back to the wigwam. There Te-Am's sister filled a basin with warm water and poured into it a sweet-smelling liquid from an earthen pot. She bathed Little Rising Sun and washed away the scars from her hands and face until her cheeks began to glow. Then she dressed her in a fine robe of soft, white buckskin that was deeply fringed and decorated with quills and beads. She brushed and combed Little Rising Sun's hair until it grew long and shiny, and she decorated it with beads and tiny shells.

When she was dressed and ready, Little Rising Sun was told to sit at the brother's side of the wigwam and to take the wife's place on the fur rug near the fire.

Scarcely was she seated when Te-Am entered. Smiling, he looked down at Little Rising Sun, saying, "Wajoolkoos – So we are found, are we?"

"Alajul aa – Yes," answered Little Rising Sun. Then Te-Am asked her to stay always in his wigwam as his wife, and his sister began to prepare the wedding feast.

Meanwhile, when the father of Little Rising Sun returned home from his hunting and found his youngest daughter gone, he asked her sisters what had become of her. "She went out," they answered, "and though we called her, she did not come back and would not obey."

The father was worried and set out to search for her. All through the village he went and finally came to the wigwam of Te-Am, where he could hear the sounds of laughter and rejoicing from within. Stepping inside he found his daughter feasting with Te-Am and his sister. At first he did not recognize his child, but then she ran to him and begged his consent to the marriage. This he gladly gave, counseling her to remain and be a good and dutiful wife. And then they all celebrated together. Little Rising Sun became the wife of the great hunter, Te-Am, and together they lived a long and happy life.

(Music: "He ga, he ga, he ga – ne he." Repeat)

Stories from the Kindergarten

In addition to finding traditional fairy tales for the kindergarten, teachers have been creating stories for their children, which draw on images from diverse cultures and include stories for special festivals. Some have appeared in the Fall 1992 issue of the *Kindergarten Newsletter*.

Teachers have also been bringing a wider variety of foods into the kindergarten. The grains themselves, which are much served in Waldorf kindergartens, come from different parts of the earth and are much associated with certain cultures.

The kindergarten teacher tries to work in such a way that the children learn through imitation rather than through instruction. When imitation prevails, the child can absorb the world deeply, more deeply than through conscious knowing. Being true to imitation is a challenge when opening the door to a wider range of cultures, for it is very tempting to make the children conscious of what is being offered. It is generally agreed that what makes a great difference is how the teacher carries this impulse. Is she self-conscious about other cultures or at ease with them? Is she trying so hard to bring other cultures to her class that it inevitably becomes a lesson better suited for the elementary school rather than a natural life-filled experience for the kindergarten? Here are examples of how two teachers are working with these thoughts in their kindergartens.

A Marionette Play for the Kindergarten

Judith Ashley, Willow Wood Educational Cooperative
Sebastopol, CA

The following story was written for a child whose father had died a few weeks before. It was told as an Indian tale, but contains a story within it of the journey back to the heavenly world on the rainbow bridge. It was presented as a table puppet play.

Once upon a time, many, many moons ago, a little boy named Shuna lived with his mother and father, his big brother, his baby sister, and his grandmother on the banks of a mighty river. His village had many tepees along its broad banks.

Every day Shuna's father and brother went out on the swift-flowing river to fish for the salmon that swam there. Shuna was not yet old enough to paddle the canoe. Instead he stayed in the village with his mother and grandmother. Mother, too, was busy every day. She and the other women of the village cut up the salmon that the braves had caught and hung it to dry on wooden racks for their winter food. Shuna's new sister rode on her mother's back, but Shuna, who was not yet old enough to cut up the fish, was often in the way. He began to spend many hours with his grandmother, wise old Kioma. She told him many stories, and he grew to love her very much. He didn't mind so much that he couldn't go on the river with his father and brother. Just hearing all the old stories filled his heart with joy. It was enough.

One day Shuna's grandmother became ill. Shuna was very worried about her. He gave her his own medicine pouch with his special crystal, his own feather, the shell he had found on the banks of the river, and the healing herbs he always wore to keep away sickness. The Shaman came, too.

(For puppet play: *He ya, He ya, He ya, He ya* – rattle)

Shuna's grandmother got well again but she did not become strong. She now spent all her time sitting in the sun, for she said that her bones were cold.

Time passed and the sun began to shine less brightly in the sky. The autumn winds began to blow, and soon even the sun did not warm Kioma's bones. Shuna became very sad. He climbed to the very top of a nearby hill and called out to Father Sun, "Oh, Father Sun, do not go away. Grandmother needs your golden rays to warm her old bones."

Father Sun pushed aside the clouds and looked down upon Shuna standing there below him, and he called down to him, "Yes, Little Shuna, soon it will be dark and cold. Such is the way of things, but I will send the last rays of my sunlight into the gorse flowers. You must pick them and weave your Grandmother a blanket of sunlight. That is sure to keep her bones warm until the days grow sunny again."

And so Shuna went along the banks of the river and picked the many gorse flowers. He lit a little fire and cooked the flowers with some of the wool from his mother's sheep. Soon he had enough of the warm yellow wool, and he ran to the village as fast as his legs would carry him until he came to the tepee of his Aunt. She was the finest weaver in the village.

"Please, Auntie," he said, "would you weave a blanket to keep Grandmother's bones warm?"

"If you will watch over my sheep," his Aunt replied, " I will set to work on it right away."

And so Shuna took up a staff and took his Aunt's sheep to feed along the grassy banks of the river. His Aunt began to weave right away and soon had woven the most beautiful blanket. It was as yellow as the summer sky, and oh, so soft. When Shuna returned, he thanked his Aunt and ran off with the blanket to show Grandmother. Gently, he wrapped it around her shoulders. Grandmother was very pleased and, though the winter winds roared outside their tepee, Grandmother stayed warm. All winter Grandmother told the stories of the old ways to Shuna. His eyes sparkled as they sat together before the fire. Sometimes he would ask her to tell him a story over and over again. And she always did.

One day Grandmother began to tell Shuna the story of the rainbow bridge. She told him how, before he had come to earth, he had lived in the sky and how he had looked over the edge of the clouds and wished he could go to earth. She told him how he had gone many, many times to the Sky Chief to ask him if he might go down the rainbow bridge, and how the Sky Chief had always said, "Not yet, it is not your time. You still have much work to do." And she told him how the little sky child had gone busily about his chores, polishing the stars until they twinkled and fluffing up the clouds. She told Shuna how the sky child had gone once again to the Sky Chief and how this time the Sky Chief had said, "Yes, child, now it is time. Your work here is done. Now it is time for you to begin your task on Earth." And he wrapped the child in a red cloak and sent him sliding down the rainbow bridge right into his mother's arms. (For puppet play, during this sentence begin humming "Huron Carol" as brown silk which covers the rainbow bridge is pulled off with a snap of the wrist so it drops instantly. Then sing "Huron Carol" while child slowly comes down the rainbow bridge.)

Shuna asked his Grandmother to tell him that story many, many times. And she always did.

Time passed, and one season followed another until once again the days began to grow short and the wind began to howl around the tepee.

Grandmother called Shuna to her. "The time has come," Kioma said, "for me to climb the rainbow bridge back to my home in the sky. My work here on Earth is finished, and the Sky Chief is calling me home. Do not feel sad for me, for I am not leaving you. Every time you tell a story, I will be with you. You have listened well. From now on you will not be called Little Shuna, but Shuna, Teller of Tales. You keep safely in your heart all the old wisdom. That is your task here on Earth. I give you back your medicine pouch, and the yellow blanket, made from the sun's last rays, will be your storytelling blanket. Wear it well." Shuna's Grandmother, wise old Kioma, turned and began to climb the rainbow bridge. (Hum "Huron Carol")

Shuna, Teller of Tales, watched until he could no longer see her, but he knew that she would always be with him. (Stop "Carol" here) And it was true, for every time Shuna, Teller of Tales, told one of the old stories he could feel his Grandmother dancing in his heart.

The Huron Carol

The "Huron Carol" is a Christmas carol originally sung in the Huron language. It was written by Father Jean de Brébeuf (1593–1649). This Jesuit missionary worked among the Huron Indians in the area where Midland, Ontario, now stands. He translated many books into the Huron language but is best remembered for telling the Christmas story in the setting of the Hurons. After an Iroquois raid, the Hurons were forced from their homes and scattered in several directions. They continued to sing the Carol in their own language, and, one hundred years later, it was translated into French and later into English.

The song is currently in print in a picture book entitled *The Huron Carol*. It was published by Dutton Children's Books in 1992, with illustrations associated with the Native American experience.

Multiculturalism in the Kindergarten

Lucia Mello, Rudolf Steiner School, NY

How one brings the spirit of multiculturalism into a kindergarten will vary tremendously according to the teacher, the community, and the ages of the children. The differences can be enormous. Here's what happens when an energetic kindergarten teacher from Brazil finds herself teaching in New York City.

I am a native South American and I teach a kindergarten class for five- and six-year-olds at the Rudolf Steiner School in New York City. When I arrived in the United States four years ago, I was impressed by the cultural diversity I encountered in New York. However, I soon found that the children in the City are not necessarily exposed to that diversity. This fact made me rethink the school's task of bringing diversity to the children and about how I could create a space in my classroom in which the children would be exposed to a diversity of cultures and therefore learn to respect and value them.

First, I think it is the teacher's responsibility to have an inner attitude of respect and reverence towards people of all cultures so the children can perceive that and imitate. I found it possible to bring diversity through preparing and cooking different foods while celebrating the festivals and through the use of daily greetings and songs in different languages.

Cooking is very much part of our routine in the kindergarten. We have tried to bake diverse types of bread from different cultures in connection with the different festivals. For example, during Thanksgiving we made a variety of Native American and South American Indian cornbreads. The children were involved in the process of grinding the corn and baking the breads. Each parent also brought a different dish that was typical of some country, and we assembled a delicious menu.

At other times we cooked potato latkes and sang Hebrew songs for Hanukkah, baked Swedish bread and cookies and sang songs for Santa Lucia's day, and we had matzo ball soup and a sweet apple and nut mixture to celebrate Passover.

Gradually, I could see the children expressing these experiences in their play. For instance, an interesting theme came out in their play which lasted for a few weeks. It was basically their own idea, and I was used to help move furniture and to be a customer for their stores which were placed side by side on a big lane which they called "All Countries Street."

Everything started because each Thursday we make soup for snack. One Thursday a boy wanted to make a Mexican bean soup, but we had no beans. Another boy suggested he should go and buy them at the store. Meanwhile, two other boys joined the play and wanted to build a market. One of them said, "They would have beans for sale!" but the other boy was determined to have a French deli, so no beans were on the shelves!

On their side, some girls were creating an Italian restaurant called "Mangia." They wanted to buy Italian goods but the boys' store carried only "French stuff." Two other girls decided to open an Italian store.

We still had the Mexican bean problem to be solved, so the chef (at this time he was wearing a chef's hat), while walking around with a big wooden spoon in his hand, decided that a Mexican store had to be opened so he could make the soup for snack. The other children got the idea. Soon, the whole classroom was involved in the project of creating their favorite food stores. Of course, someone already had beans, hot peppers, tostados and tacos in their cargo ship coming direct from Mexico. Later that cargo ship became a Japanese store.

After a while, all the kindergarten props were imaginatively used as international goods. All the workers were fed by the Italian restaurant, which was surrounded by a row of international stores: a Japanese store with sushi; beside it a French deli with all kinds of French food and wine; the Spanish store sold ingredients for the Mexican soup; an Italian grocery supplied everyone with pastas of all types and styles; an American sports store was opened for the camping and hiking explorers, as well as for the cowboys; and an African-American store sold musical instruments with "wooden drums of all kinds."

My role was to come to each store and buy ingredients for our snack, and I was expected to speak the native language spoken in the country of each store. That was the most fun for the children. I came to each one and greeted them in their language and asked for the food I wanted. Luckily I speak Portuguese and Spanish, and a little Italian and French. For the Japanese shop I knew only a few words, but that was good enough for the children. In the African store I communicated by singing a song I knew in a dialect and made the gestures of playing a drum.

This whole theme was sustained but transformed a little every day. As a whole, the theme is still there. Sometimes it becomes more apparent, sometimes less, just like the natural breathing rhythm of the group.

Waldorf in the Public Sector

Ann Pratt, Urban Waldorf Program, Milwaukee, WI

This is an excerpt of an article from the 1993 Spring/Summer issue of the AWSNA Newsletter and describes the first Waldorf public school program in the United States. Its students come from the inner city and other neighborhoods and are mostly of African-American background. In a conversation with Ann Pratt, facilitator at the school, she said the Urban faculty is developing curriculum materials which they hope to share with other Waldorf teachers in future issues of this Multicultural Journal.

About the World

The sky is blue
The grass is green
Pink, purple, green and red
are the colors seen.

Black is for our skin
Green is for our land
Red is for our blood
As we join hand in hand.

– Brandon Burton, 5th grade

This poem, written by one of our fifth graders at the Urban Waldorf School, is one example of how our children are beginning to feel and express what we have been making an effort to engender in them: a recognition of the strength of their heritage. As a faculty, we are working on our multicultural curriculum from many aspects. From this spring on into the fall, we will concentrate on the African-American culture, including a study tracing how the Blacks came to our area, initially from the west coast of Africa as slaves and eventually up the Mississippi. As part of this, the faculty will also study one country in Africa, Ghana, with the purpose of absorbing as many aspects of an African culture as possible. Our aim is to bring a multilevel experience to our school as a whole in order to help our children feel and recognize their roots. We are finding many ways to incorporate African mythology, folk stories, poems and songs into main lessons where appropriate.

Our teachers have also begun to incorporate aspects of Native American cultures, which are especially appropriate in third and fourth grades. We are working actively with the Waldorf curriculum, holding to it throughout the grades. Our struggle is how to find a right balance. It is engaging and completely absorbing work that will take time to refine, but we are launched.

Another important aspect of our work involves the parents. Several parents mentioned how the "depression" their children had experienced in other school situations has disappeared. One of the children told her mother she could now throw away her dark-colored crayons, as she didn't need them anymore. Many of our teachers now are returning from their internships (with experienced Waldorf teachers) filled with new inspiration, and yet there is the sobering reality of the many problems that our children bring to school. Perhaps it is best summed up in Principal Dorothy St. Charles' phrase: "This is the happiest group of hurting children I have ever seen."

Multicultural Resources

Picture Books of Interest

Although Waldorf kindergartens prefer to tell stories rather than read them, the following titles are offered with parents in mind, for they often seek advice on books. Our thanks to Terry Dammann of the Washington Waldorf School Library for her write-ups on favorite books and to Linda Atamian of Pond Meadow Home Day Care in Rhode Island for hers. Some of the books may be better suited for grade school children than for kindergarten children.

Bang, Molly, *The Paper Crane*, Greenwillow Books

One day a penniless stranger enters a restaurant and asks for food. The owner serves him generously—and receives a mysterious, magical reward. Evocative words and striking three-dimensional paper sculpture illustrations make this another very special book from Molly Bang. (5–8)

De Paola, Tomie, *The Legend of the Bluebonnet*

Based on a Comanche legend, this is the story of an orphan Indian girl who sacrifices her most prized possession to benefit her drought-stricken tribe. De Paola's pictures convey the beauty and sparseness of the Texas hills.

**Grammer, Maurine, "The Gift of Colored Corn"
in *The Bear That Turned White and Other Native Tales*,
Northland Publishing**

This is a San Juan Pueblo tale reminiscent of familiar fairy tales.

San Souci, Robert, *Sukey and the Mermaid*, Four Winds Press

In this African-American tale set in South Carolina, Sukey lives with her ma and step-pa, "Mister Hard Times." She runs off from her work to a secret place by the sea and she meets Mama Jo, a beautiful black mermaid. (Linda Atamian writes: We did this as a puppet play with table puppets and a marionette for Mama Jo. It is probably more fitting for the first grade than kindergarten.)

San Souci, Robert, *The Talking Eggs*, Dial Books for Young Readers

Children will be spellbound by this unique and colorful folk tale of the American South. It is the story of two sisters, Blanche and Rose, one spoiled and lazy, the other good and sweet. Blanche is miserable until one day her kindness to an old witch woman catapults her into a strange world—strangest of all are the talking eggs, which dramatically prove that beauty may hide great ugliness, while plain objects may contain treasures.(5–8)

Steptoe, John, *Mufaro's Beautiful Daughters*, Lothrop

In creating a modern fable about two sisters with opposite natures, Steptoe employs richly colored scenes individualized by expressive faces and dramatic backgrounds. (5–7)

Winter, Jeanette, *Follow the Drinking Gourd*, Knopf

Remarkable pictures that spring directly from American folk tradition and a text that weaves history and song together combine in this moving story of a conductor on the Underground Railroad and a band of slaves who follow the drinking gourd to freedom. (5–7)

**Wolkstein, Diane, *The Magic Wings, A Tale from China,*
Puffin Unicorn Book (hb) and E.P. Dutton (pb)**

A little goose girl longs to fly. She is joined by the grocer's daughter, the judge's daughter, the Princess and the Queen. It is told as a sequential tale.

Bibliographies and Sources

The Black Experience in Children's Books is an annotated bibliography printed by the New York Public Library, 455 Fifth Avenue, New York, NY 10018.

A bibliography of books recommended for a greater multicultural awareness was compiled by the class of 1991 at the Washington Waldorf School, 4800 Sangamore Rd., Bethesda, MD 20816. The school hopes to update the list in the summer and have it available for distribution in the fall.

Mail order firms which specialize in multicultural books, toys and other materials:

Integrity Books, Cards and Prints, 116 West Wright St, Milwaukee, WI 53212. Phone (414) 264-6215.

Maral Enterprises, P.O. Box 361, New York, NY 10028. Phone (212) 348-7080.

Claudia's Caravan, P.O. Box 1582, Alameda, CA 94501.

For books by Rudolf Steiner or others on Waldorf education or anthroposophy, contact Waldorf Publications, 38 Main Street, Chatham, NY, 12037, www.waldorfpublications.org.

Numerous resource books and articles are also available at the Online Waldorf Library (OWL) at www.waldorflibrary.org.

The Rudolf Steiner Library has a large collection of fairy tale books (with a printed list of what's available) as well as books on many other subjects. For information, contact the library at 351 Fairview Ave., Ste 610, Hudson, NY 12534, www.anthroposophy.org/library, email rsteinerlibrary@gmail.com.

In Appreciation

Contributors: Joan Almon, Judith Ashley, Kristi Busch, Susan
Cook, Arvia MacKaye Ege, Nancy Foster, Barbara Francis,
Elaine Harris, Susan Howard, Keith Jefferson, Janet
Kellman, Monica Marshall, Russell Meek, Lucia Mello,
David Mitchell, Irene Morgan, Che Norman, Ann Pratt,
Ann Rainville, Ann Rose, Betty Staley, Jim Staley, Manette
Teitelbaum

Daniel Bittleston, for his photograph of the Max Stibbe School

Clopper Almon, Carol Petrash and Lydia Roberson for editorial
assistance